INNOVATION NATION

Affinity Press
New York, New York

affinitypressbooks.com

ISBN 10: 1499364229
ISBN 13: 978-1499364224

INNOVATION NATION

TOWARD A RIGHT-LEFT ALLIANCE

TO UNLEASH AMERICA'S CREATIVE CAPACITY

AND ENTREPRENEURIAL ENERGY

Ten Principles to Empower **REAL PEOPLE**
and Small Business and Government
for Jobs, Clean Energy, Low Taxes,
and **REAL PROSPERITY**

Includes

THE 3% SOLUTION: A NEW LEADERSHIP ROLE FOR BUSINESS

BY BILL SHIREMAN

CONTENTS

INNOVATION NATION

EXECUTIVE SUMMARY

America has grown addicted to debt. So severe is our dependency that even in the face of successive economic crises, our predictable response is to simply take on new forms of debt—financial, social, and environmental—and delay the day of reckoning. The Left and Right point fingers at one another, but neither has offered a viable way out.

We simply can't pay down our debts by radically cutting back, drilling ever more oil and gas, or shifting costs to the environment or the future—the costs of overreaction are too high. But so too are the costs of inaction. It is time to stop living on debt, and to create value instead.

Fortunately, creating value is one of the things America does best. Our people have the creativity, enterprise, and technological capacity.

Last century we drove more than a 14-fold improvement in labor productivity.[1] This century, our people and technologies give us the capacity to improve energy and resource productivity

---

1 U.S. Bureau of Labor Statistics. 1890 to 1949, from Historical Statistics of the United States, Series D 683-688, "Indexes of Employee Output", 1869 to 1969; 1949 to 1987, from U.S. Bureau of Labor Statistics, http://www.bls.gov/lpc/ "Industry analytical ratios for the manufacturing, all persons" Superseded historical SIC measures for manufacturing, durable manufacturing, and nondurable manufacturing sectors, 1949-2003 ftp://ftp.bls.gov/pub/special.requests/opt/lpr/histmfgsic.zip; 1987 to 2007, from U.S. Bureau of Labor Statistics, http://www.bls.gov/lpc/, Series Id: PRS30006092, 1987 to 2007. Year 1890 was set equal to 100. See also Professor Richard D. Wolff, http://rdwolff.com/content/keynesian-revival-marxian-critique

ten-fold, step-by-step and leap-by-leap, at an average rate of at least 3 percent per year.[2]

Labor Productivity from 1890 to 2009

3% Resource Productivity Increase 2009 to 2105

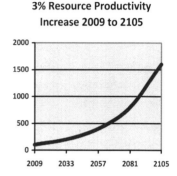

Achieving that objective—driving a 3 percent annual gain in total productivity—would not only pay off our economic debts, but also develop technologies that open a path to prosperity for the world's developing nations, all while sustaining energy and water supplies, and reducing U.S carbon and other pollutants more than 75 percent in half a century. Innovation would enable us to have, do, and be much more, while consuming, polluting, and wasting much less.

This path of innovation plays to our strengths—to the ingenuity of our people, and to the potential of the information-based technologies in which we lead the world.

---

2 World Wildlife Fund, with McKinsey and Company and CDP, The 3% Solution, 2013, see https://worldwildlife.org/projects/the-3-solution; McKinsey Global Institute, Resource Revolution, 2011, see http://www.mckinsey.com/insights/energy_resources_materials/resource_revolution; and McKinsey Global Institute, Growth and Renewal in the United States: Retooling America's Economic Engine, February 2011 (James Manyika, David Hunt, Scott Nyquist, Jaana Remes, Vikram Malhotra, Lenny Mendonca, Byron Auguste, and Samantha Test.)

But neither big government nor big corporations will lead this revolution. We won't find innovation along a hard path dominated by commands-and-controls that lock us into past business models or social roles. Innovation involves the generation of new ideas and knowledge that lead to changes in products, processes, services, organizations, and cultures—and these changes are almost always resisted by status quo interests.

Instead, innovation is most likely to take root on soft ground receptive to the creative capacities of people, and the economic and social entrepreneurism of small institutions. Big business and big government will benefit from the shift, and they too will thrive in the long run, but they will not control the change.

The payoffs are significant. A 3 percent annual improvement in resource productivity can pay down our debts, enable rising prosperity here and abroad,[3] and protect the oceans, forests, and the atmosphere that support life.

If we fail, however, the costs will be heavy. We may set ourselves up for the kind of hard-path non-solutions favored by extremists and ideologues on all sides. We may lurch from one surrender to another—surrendering freedom to impose excessive controls on enterprise, surrendering prosperity to pay off debts too quickly, surrendering the environment to finance one last illusory growth spurt, or surrendering tomorrow to finance business-as-usual today.

To successfully walk the path to innovation, we must break the political gridlock that cements in place the policies of a bygone era, a proud era that has served its purpose. The resource-intensive industrial economy of the last century created unprecedented prosperity. But it also planted the seeds of its

---

3 McKinsey Global Institute, Growth and Renewal in the United States: Retooling America's Economic Engine, February 2011

successor—an economy that can grow more value with less consumption.

People don't need to be subsidized by government or commanded by corporations to create value. Those capacities lie within them and between them, waiting to be brought to life. All we need do is support the cultivation and development of creative potentials, by nesting them in a framework of laws that reward innovation while assuring that negative externalities are owned, that responsibilities are taken seriously, that we are good stewards. In this way, when people create value, the rewards accrue to themselves, their families, their nation and the world.

To overcome our debts and start creating value again, an America dedicated to innovation would advance ten principles:

1. SET A NATIONAL GOAL. Target a 3% annual gain in overall productivity in public policy, not as a singular mandate, but as a target to guide our progress.

2. SET SECTOR GOALS. Leading companies in each sector set their own goals, in consultation with experts and stakeholders, that support 3% national gain.

3. UNLEASH PEOPLE. Cut public and private barriers to individual enterprise, especially small business and microenterprise

4. REFORM TAXES. Stop taxing jobs, growth, and prosperity—tax pollution instead

5. WIND DOWN SUBSIDIES. Stop subsidizing the past—wean us off unnecessary spending

6. INCREASE RESEARCH. Fund R&D for the future—especially basic and applied research with broad multi-sector benefits—to drive both incremental and breakthrough resource gains

7. PROTECT AIR, WATER, AND LAND. Reduce environmental and climate risks, and use the market to foster conservation and stewardship, such as through prices on pollution

8. RENEW CITIES AND COMMUNITIES. Reform outdated codes and end barriers to small business, microenterprise, and the sharing economy to revitalize big cities, small towns, and local communities

9. REFORM GOVERNANCE. Move beyond gridlock, toward government that is democratic, accessible, functional, and free

10. INCLUDE EVERYONE. Celebrate the capacities of all people in all their diversity, respecting and welcoming women and men, gay and straight, minorities and majorities to contribute fully, without prejudice

In an Innovation Nation—a nation that embraces change and harnesses it to advantage—the Right and Left can work functionally together to cultivate genuine long-term prosperity. They can apply core principles from both sides of the political spectrum. Stepping only to the right, or only to the left, we walk in circles. But by stepping right, then left, then right and left again, we move ahead.

Breaking America's Addiction to Debt

No False Panaceas, Right or Left

Conservatives are right: as a nation, we are out of money and deep in debt. Progressives are also right: we cannot pay off our debt by extracting it from the poor, the middle class, or the environment.

But many Right and Left leaders are wrong about what to do. To stimulate new growth, many on the Right believe it is enough to simply *drill baby drill* the nation's limited energy resources, as fast as we can, while many on the Left propose that we simply *spend baby spend* financial resources the nation does not have, as fast as we can, and then pay off our growing debts by printing more money. Together, both are content to drill-and-spend, as a "compromise" that satisfies the interest groups that influence them.

These are false panaceas. The Right and Left often overlook a simple fact: there is a difference between spending money and earning money. Neither government nor the planet is an ATM machine with an infinite balance. As we draw down on our wealth, we need to build it up as well, and restore our balance.

The real answer to this dilemma is not to consume value. It is to create it, by tapping the creativity and enterprise of people, including their capacity to innovate.

But institutional forces are arrayed heavily against change, because they have grown so reliant on American consumers to overspend when called upon, to support a global system of finance that is badly out of balance. As Professor Larry Diamond of Stanford University said in 2010, "We basically have two bankrupt parties bankrupting the country."

Before the economic crisis of 2008, Americans liquidated their individual and collective assets at an extraordinary rate, each American spending an average of $120 a day that they mostly didn't have, for an array of things they mostly didn't need, made by people thousands of miles away of whom they mostly had no knowledge, connection, or concern.

America's debt-financed consumption binge is what supported growth across the global economy, up to the moment that crisis hit. Our nation was slowly but systematically transferring trillions of dollars in debt, to often-adversarial nations with little attachment to free democratic institutions, in exchange for cheap products and resources in quantities we couldn't afford.

Within four months of the crisis, America's per capita spending plunged to just $44 a day. Six years later, we are still struggling to raise that to $90 a day.[4] Whether we can afford it or not, the world "needs" us to step forward, with our dollars in hand, to keep precipitous decline at bay, and push forward a bit further the day when our accounts come due.

The debt cycle is unnecessary. We have the capacity for a robust economy founded on actual value creation. But our institutions have grown so dependent on instruments of debt that we delay the modest shifts needed to generate sustainable

---

4 Roy Spence, co-founder, GSDM, April, 2014.

wealth, in favor of an illusion that allows us to insulate the status quo from needed change.

Economist Bruce Bartlett, a senior policy advisor to the Reagan and George H. W. Bush administrations, has grown weary of the false debate. In his 2011 book, "The Benefit and the Burden: Tax Reform—Why We Need It and What It Will Take," he describes the futility of massive cuts in federal spending.

Bartlett points out that based on 2011 Treasury Department data, the government's total indebtedness now stands at over $51.3 trillion. The national debt made up a fifth of this—$10.2 trillion. Veterans and federal employees are owed $5.8 trillion. Social Security's unfunded liability—promised benefits over expected Social Security revenues—is $9.2 trillion over the next 75 years. And Medicare's unfunded liability is $24.6 trillion.

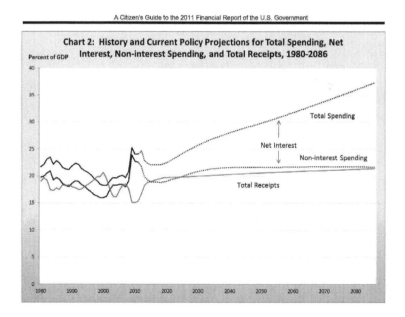

A Citizen's Guide to the 2011 Financial Report of the U.S. Government

Chart 2: History and Current Policy Projections for Total Spending, Net Interest, Non-interest Spending, and Total Receipts, 1980-2086

If a corporation accumulated debt of this magnitude, it would be forced to report it on an accrual basis, forcing it into bankruptcy. But because the federal government operates on a cash basis, it can ignore for the time being the vast amount of debt we face to fulfill political commitments we have made to important constituencies: future benefits to retired federal employees, veterans, and Social Security and Medicare recipients. These must be paid only when they come due, so they do not appear in the federal budget, and are almost never counted when we measure the government debt.

Ignoring the debt doesn't make it go away—it just means the bill will come due suddenly, and perhaps unpredictably, in the form of future economic crises. Whether the crises comes next year or next generation, whether they come by economic or political force, they will have a devastating financial impact on the nation.

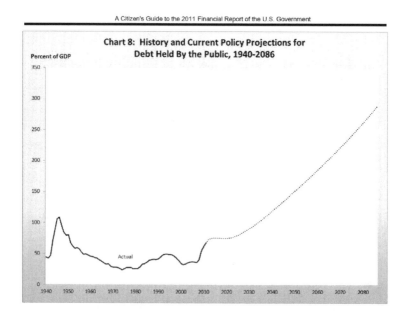

Chart 8: History and Current Policy Projections for Debt Held By the Public, 1940-2086

Balancing the federal budget will not be nearly enough to reduce the risk, as Bartlett and other economists document. The federal government would have to run a substantial surplus continuously for 75 years just to prevent the debt to GDP ratio from rising.

If we cannot cut spending enough to erase the debt, what can we do? The first instinct of many on the Right has been to do what worked during our last period of continuous growth in the mid-1900s: consume more fossil fuel energy.

But that path is well worn. It has been almost forty years since the first global energy crisis in 1973. Since that time, rather than innovating beyond our dependence on fossil fuels, we focused on building our military power, enabling us to intervene, to protect our sources of supply and prevent disruptions. We have as a consequence sacrificed $7 trillion in domestic growth, to fund our foreign oil habit. We have transferred over $1.2 trillion to nations that are either unstable or antithetical to our interests. Those dollars financed the Baathist terrorists under Saddam Hussein in Iraq, the radical Mullahs under the Ayatollah in Iran, and of course Al Qaeda and the Mujahedeen with their roots in Saudi Arabia. In Saudi Arabia, the first Al Qaeda terrorists were so infuriated by the presence of US military on Saudi soil, that they focused their oil-financed operation on throwing the infidels off their soil. Then, failing that, they came to our soil. They used a few of their oil dollars to buy airline tickets in 2001, and took out the World Trade Center, and along with it 3,000 lives.

The other panacea of some is to drill our way out of debt. Thanks to recent improvements in hydrological fracturing technology, the U.S. can now access vast holdings of natural gas, enough to largely replace our highly polluting stocks of coal, which are being depleted more quickly than once thought. The huge increase in available natural gas has driven prices down to a fraction of global levels. It has also enabled the U.S. to reduce reliance on coal, which has driven the nation's carbon emissions back to 1992 levels.

But hydrological fracturing, while important to both the economy and environment, is no panacea. Economic costs of unconventional gas and oil are proving much higher than many anticipated. Today's low prices reflect temporary oversupply, and shield consumers and manufacturers from high underlying production costs. Keeping prices this low would require that we continue to produce at high levels, exclusively for domestic markets, even though prices can't support the costs. This isn't likely, but even if it were to somehow be mandated, it would represent a costly subsidy that would perpetuate a false price signal. We would again be subsidizing growth with debt, rather than creating value.

Domestic oil production is also experiencing a boom. Yet oil prices hit record highs in 2012, as did OPEC oil revenues. Our costs of extracting fuels in North America are simply too high to compete in a wellhead-to-wellhead match-up. The OPEC oil cartel sits on 78 percent of conventional oil reserves, and it caps production at a third of global supply. As analysts Anne Korin and Gal Luft note, they continue to engineer global supply to support their political objectives. "When we drill more, they drill less, and when we use less, they drill less. It's time to change the paradigm."[5]

More than two-thirds of the oil we use is for transportation; 97 percent of U.S. transportation energy is based on petroleum. Between 2006 and 2013, U.S. imports fell from over 60 percent of our supply need to 45 percent, yet our expenditures on imports increased, not just per barrel but in total.[6]

---

5 http://setamericafree.org/

6 *Ibid.*

In short, OPEC can outlast us. The U.S. still consumes a quarter of the world's oil supply, and even with our newfound bounty, we hold as little as 3 percent of global oil reserves.[7] We cannot drill our way out of our energy problem. We don't own enough oil.

Given this power dynamic, it would be imprudent for the U.S. to unilaterally liquidate this newly-found bounty. While fossil fuels may be plentiful here right now, the most plentiful oil reserves we can afford to extract are still in the hands of Middle Eastern regimes: Saudi Arabia, Iraq, Iran, UAE, Kuwait, and Libya, and their low production costs will continue to give them powerful leverage over global markets.

Korin and Luft, the scholars who lead the Right-to-Left alliance called *Set America Free*, note that with oil rising from $25 to over $100 per barrel in just six years, oil-rich countries have more than quadrupled their revenues, bringing in over $1 trillion in revenues in 2013 alone. "The resulting transfer of wealth is already creating a structural shift in the global economy, creating economic fallout such as swollen trade deficits, loss of jobs, sluggish economic growth, inflation and, if prices continue to soar, inevitable recessions. At today's prices, foreign oil producers are extracting a tax of more than $1,600 a year from every American man, woman and child. In 2007, over $50 billion of local, state and federal taxes were lost to foreign oil. In 2007, our dependency on foreign oil deprived the U.S. of over one million jobs, they write.[8]

If oil prices reach $200 a barrel, the levels some predict, OPEC could potentially buy Bank of America with one month's production, and Apple Computers in a week. It would take less

---

7 *Ibid.*

8 *Ibid.*

than two years of production for OPEC to own a 20 percent stake in every S&P 500 company.[9]

If they bide their time and maintain authoritarian rule, Middle East producers can outlast Russia, Mexico, Norway, China, Brazil, and even the U.S. If we don't innovate, the Middle East this century could an even bigger share of global oil reserves than before.

In the long term, both our supply of fossil fuels and the environment's capacity to sustain emissions is limited. It would be better to consider our energy resources for what they are—a bank account we can tap over time, not a one-time lottery winning to be spent in a few years.

Much as some on the Right might wish, it is impossible to drill enough oil or cut enough spending to pay our debt. Much as the Left might wish, it is impossible to just print more money, and erase the paper debt as it comes due. The reality that neither side may wish to face is this: we simply cannot spend our way to prosperity. It is impossible to live off windfalls and subsidies forever. Eventually, someone has to create real value.

9 *Ibid.*

CREATING VALUE AGAIN:

Toward America's Second Productivity Revolution

In a world where more than a billion people across Europe, Asia, and the Americas now enjoy materially prosperous lives, it is easy to forget that in all civilizations and social orders before America, "the vast bulk of humanity had been preoccupied with responding to basic material needs," as Brink Lindsey writes. America's singular achievement in the 20th century was unleashing productive powers "far beyond anything in prior human experience."[10]

To end the Depression and win World War II, the federal government harnessed business to build the engine that powered America's ascendance. Our free enterprise system, combined with economic, monetary and tax policies explicitly designed to expand our productive capacities, enabled America to out-produce the Axis powers and win the war, meet exploding postwar demand for housing and consumer products, reconstruct Europe and Japan, and ultimately outlast the Soviet Union and win the Cold War. In the process, the size and scope of both government and the corporate sector reached new heights.

---

10 Brink Lindsey, The Age of Abundance, http://store.cato.org/books/age-abundance-how-prosperity-transformed-americas-politics-culture-hardback

Today, America's great global project is no longer to help defeat Fascism, stop communism, or produce goods for all the world's middle class consumers. Rather, the grand strategy that perhaps best advances both our interests and those of the world is to drive a new innovation revolution that will not only enable Americans to prosper in a new era, but invite an additional three billion aspirants to join the global middle class, in just two short decades—without experiencing resource wars, insurgencies, and the devastation of our planet's ecosystem.

We have the capacity to do so. In the hands of a creative and free people, today's emerging technologies enable us step-by-step to draw forth more of the creative capacity in people, while using a fraction of the resources required in the century past.

But to cultivate the prosperous, sustainable, value-creating economy that is within our reach, we need to begin to break some old habits that used to serve us well, but now threaten to undermine not just our capacity to grow a new middle class, but to preserve the one that today's prosperous billion enjoy.

To win wars both hot and cold in the 20th century and build the world's richest economy, the U.S. drove a revolution in labor productivity, where in just over a century we multiplied 14-fold the amount of value generated for every hour of labor worked.

Barriers to this innovation revolution were swept away in large part by depression and war, which made it clear to all that change was essential to survival. Innovation involves the generation of new ideas and knowledge that lead to changes in products, processes, services, organizations, and cultures—and these changes are almost always resisted by status quo interests, except at moments of crisis and potential collapse.

The engines that drove our last productivity revolution were, quite literally, engines, and the machines they powered. The industrial machine age enabled America and much of the world to overcome a labor shortage that stood in the way of global prosperity, and raise living standards for the vast majority of our people.

The institutions that ran those machines were huge and centralized. People voluntarily traded some of their independence and autonomy, to secure the freedom and prosperity enabled by our productive capacities. They came to rely on big government and big corporations—who themselves also grew increasingly large and interdependent.

But the world has changed, thanks largely to ideas and technologies that reverse the flow of power. Today, the new engines of prosperity are *thinking* machines—microchips, computers, cell phones, and a myriad knowledge-embedded products and services. And the new institutions that tap their potential are often not big and centrally controlled. Increasingly, they are small and quick moving, or big but decentralized, because by empowering people and enabling change, they prosper more.

The core attribute of these thinking machines, and the more open enterprises that create and use them, is their capacity to not just raise labor productivity, but the productivity of all resources: energy, water, land, materials, and the hearts, minds and muscles of people. This quality can enable us to support higher levels of both freedom and prosperity, for ourselves and billions more, without exhausting our economic and ecological support systems.

Our challenge and opportunity this century is to nearly match the last era's productivity gains, bringing forward all the creative capacities of our people, so that we generate about ten times more economic value for every unit of energy and raw materials we use.

The task sounds daunting, yet it is well within reach. We achieved it with labor productivity; we can do the same again. All that is needed is the will to pursue what is in our own national and global best interest, and to shift to a 21st century version of the policy framework that shaped last century's growth and prosperity.

Given the scale of today's economic and ecological debt, it may be hard to remember that America's wealth was built on the *creation* of value. From the outset of World War II until the early 1970s, we built and deployed the world's most productive economy, creating enough surplus value to raise our prosperity while winning wars both hot and cold.

To create value and deliver it to people, America's 20th century economy combined the technical skills of scientists and engineers, with the executive skills of managers and leaders, and the hard work of millions of 9-to-5 workers in large centralized corporate enterprises, to generate unprecedented wealth.

But during the 1970s, we began to cross the line from a *value*-creating economic model to a *debt*-creating one. Suffering the costs of two energy crises in the 1970s brought on by closely-held supplies of our core fuels, we began to insulate our economy from the genuine costs of our consumption.

Instead of relying on market forces to drive innovation and adaptation, we pursued the politically expedient path of cloaking the costs of consumption, using a combination of fiscal, monetary, and regulatory policy of the past.

This shifted the source of prosperity from innovation and enterprise to debt-financed production and consumption. Keynesian-style spending practices designed for economic crises became standard political practice even when the economy was healthy. Institutions that were already big grew even bigger;

power was further consolidated; individual autonomy was lessened in these organizations.

Innovation was not halted, however. Indeed, even though we effectively subsidized consumption and debt, the 1970s saw explosive growth in the information sector, as microchips began to revolutionize the way we created value, toppling the first in a series of dominoes, disrupting each and every high-consumption industrial archetype, and redefining products, processes, factories, stores, jobs, nations, and lives.

The core technologies of the information era drove significant gains in productivity, especially within the economic silos where they originated—gains not of an incremental percent or two, but leapfrog advances that often reached 100 percent, 1000 percent, or more.

Along the way, they also imposed a healthy dose of change on the large institutions that dominated the last phase of growth. They cultivated change, empowered people, and occasionally disrupted whole sectors, as they introduced new and often radically more productive ways to deliver value to people.

THE ENERGY PRODUCTIVITY EXPLOSION

Year	The Innovation	Productivity Gain	What It Enabled	What It Disabled
1960	PACKET-SWITCHING in data transmission	1000%	Arpanet	Circuit-switching and PBX for data and, later, voice
1969	ARPANET, predecessor of the Internet	300%	Routers, LANs, faster and better university research	
1974	ETHERNET	100,000%	Internet	
1974	INTEL 8080 MICRO-PROCESSOR	10,000%	Personal Computer	Mainframe Computer
1975	ALTAIR PERSONAL COMPUTER	100,000%	Apple II	
1977	APPLE II	100%	Internet and, later, VOIP	IBM
1980s	INTERNET	Immeasurable	World Wide Web	Experts and Reference Desks
1993	WWW	Immeasurable	Email	Post Office
1993	AOL EMAIL	Immeasurable	Commerce	Brick-and-Mortar
1995	AMAZON AND E-BAY	Major	Social Media	Print Media
2000s	SKYPE AND VOIP	Major	Free Long Distance and Video Calls	International Long Distance
2000s	BLOGS, FACEBOOK, TWITTER	Major	Transparency and People Power	Privacy and Institutional Power

22

THE ENERGY PRODUCTIVITY
EXPLOSION

Through the turn of the 20th Century, energy productivity gains for specific activities led to overall gains in economic productivity. Yet the gains were limited. We had the capacity to create more value, but our increasingly obsolete fiscal, tax, and monetary policies kept productivity growth well below rates of debt accumulation.

Today, even as energy productivity continues to increase within the information and telecommunications sector, overall productivity growth is being constrained by a framework of policies and institutions designed for another era.

If we can set ourselves free from the constraints of a debt-and-consumption dependent economy, the net effect could be another economic transformation as great as the transition from the agricultural age to the industrial age and as great as the already dramatic transition from the industrial age to the early information age. The real potential lies in the shift from an industrial economy *refined* by information, as exemplified by virtual storefronts like Amazon, toward a truly new economy *founded* on it—a place where industry is simply part of a new system that transcends it, just as agriculture is part of the industrial world today. As Henry Jenkins, founder and director of the Comparative Media Studies Program at MIT, says, "For those of you keeping score, the dotcom era has ended.... We are no longer talking about interactive media technologies; we are talking about *participatory culture.* "[11]

Unfortunately, while the rapid growth of digital games, gadgets, and products suggest that innovation is robust, our rates of underlying value creation are still far below what they need to be, to generate the sustainable prosperity needed to support our existing middle class, much less the billions of others who seek prosperity alongside us. We are adapting around the edges of the debt economy, but not moving to create real net value.

The full benefits of innovation have so far been repressed by a series of policy decisions and, more important, non-decisions, that have locked the economy into a debt-financed consumerist mode, even when we have the capacity to grow much more, and consume much less.

When a particular course of action leads to unparalleled levels of prosperity, it is easy to understand why we might wish to perpetuate it, even accelerate it. But consumption was not the cause of American prosperity—it was the consequence. The genius of America was not our capacity to extract, burn, and consume more fossil fuels and raw materials—it was our capacity to unleash the creative and productive powers of a free and enterprising people, to set them loose to meet and overcome an extraordinary challenge.

Instead of tapping the creative capacities of people, we still retain an outdated policy frame designed for relatively generic mass workers and consumers, remarkably alike in tastes and lifestyles, to drive physical expansion in which their chief responsibility was not to create wealth but to maximize consumption. We forgot that living *within* our means is the best

11 Jenkins, Henry. YouTube to YouNiversity. USC Annenberg Center Speaker Series (2007). See http://www.youtube.com/watch?v=ardhuq677cU

way to *expand* our means, and foster the innovations that create genuine growth. Instead, we chose to soften the feedback signals that could have enhanced the flow of innovation and adaptation.

We still use a combination of economic and ecological debt financing to drive net-loss consumerism. Economically, we artificially drive consumption higher through unprecedented levels of household, corporate, and federal debt, to finance purchases of more consumer goods, mostly from far beyond our borders.

Then we further conceal the costs of the debt through accommodative monetary policies, which sink interest rates almost to zero, making it appear that borrowing is virtually risk-free—that the smartest course of action is to put off to tomorrow the changes we could readily make today.

We pretend that easy money will lead to more investment and, eventually, genuine growth. But absent a compelling driver for innovation and change, companies and consumers opt instead for more of the same—more spending now, on the same stuff as before, with a tiny proportion shaved off for genuine innovation.

Ecologically, we artificially drive consumption by concealing the present and future costs of resource consumption, effectively subsidizing pollution and waste, even at the expense of the earth's natural systems—the air, water, land, forests, and oceans on which we depend for our lives and livelihoods.

We need these systems to be healthy, if we are to achieve the factor 10 gains in productivity necessary to support and expand our own middle class and welcome three billion more people to the global middle class buffet. Without productivity gains, we will continue to strip the environment of the resources we need for the long term. Without a healthy ocean we will lack the sustainable fisheries to feed protein to our children. Without ample clean water we will lack the productive farms necessary to feed people, much less livestock. Without a stable and predictable climate, we will be forced to expend trillions to adapt to atmospheric shifts whose consequences cannot be fully predicted.

Yet politically, we remain locked into the tax, subsidy, and regulatory priorities of a prior age, slowing the rate of innovation needed to emulate last century's productivity leap.

Abroad, other major economies are imprudently following our lead. Driven by consumer spending propped up by debt, they are doubling down on the old system, exacerbating trade imbalances and driving record resource extraction. As commodity prices rise, global powers are hedging ever more aggressively—stockpiling resources and increasingly becoming entangled in conflicts in resource-rich areas. As the global economy falters, unrest rises and the great unresolved conflicts of the 20th century—the Middle East, South Asia, North Korea, Taiwan—grow increasingly enmeshed in the power dynamics of this new era.

Simply put, the current U.S. and international order is unsustainable, and myriad disruptions signal that it is now in a process of decline, with a potential for collapse. Until the dysfunctional U.S. political system adopts a new global mission more in alignment with the needs of the century ahead, the country risks increasingly serious degradation of domestic and global conditions.

Even with our efforts to use debt to repress key feedback signals, we are still making positive strides. The new technologies of a post-consumerist economy are so much more productive than those of the last century that they can sometimes overcome the fiscal and monetary policies that restrain them. The enterprising natures of our people—the creative and productive energies of scientists, engineers, designers, artists, and people expressing all their qualities—are disrupting old machine-age business models and bringing more profitable and sustainable successors into being, leading to the creation of new value.

Market forces are both attracting and compelling businesses to adapt to new ideas, technologies, and cultural preferences. It is not always virtue so much as necessity that is motivating business leadership. Business is stepping forward, sometimes enthusiastically, sometimes willingly, and sometimes reluctantly.

But business leaders need to do more, not just for the public interest but for their own. It is tempting to simply stand by status quo interests, through generic policy intermediaries such as trade associations, chambers of commerce, and K-Street government affairs units, whose stock-in-trade is protecting existing assets by vetoing policy innovation. These institutions represent important interests, but they err toward the interests of the past, not the future. They drive consumption and debt-creation, not innovation and value-creation. They empower large centralized institutions, not the individuals and small enterprises that are the wellspring of value creation.

Business leaders must supplement traditional government affairs efforts, through institutions that focus attention on the interests of the future. These institutions too will be decidedly pro-enterprise, but in a manner that also assures the health of the systems, small-scale institutions, large shareholders and disperse stakeholders whose well-being are interconnected with those of commerce.

The deadlocked political class will not be able to lead, until they have the support of forward-thinking business leaders who can collectively advance not just individual companies and industries, but an innovative, resilient, and sustainable economy.

This is not an over-the-horizon imperative. We together face five distinct challenges, and we must begin to engage them now. If we can meet them, they will become opportunities with generous bottom line payoffs for people, companies, and communities. But if we delay, they will become heavy liabilities, perhaps threatening not just trapped capital and quarterly earnings, but the health of America's economy, democracy, and freedom.[12]

The first of these challenges is the nation's Debt Dependency, which takes both economic and non-economic forms. The need is fundamental. As noted earlier, the federal government's total indebtedness now stands at more than $51.3 trillion, based on the U.S. Treasury Department's *Financial Report of the United States Government (December 2011)*. This debt totals nearly the entire net worth of all American households. We are literally broke—out of money. It would be impossible to cut spending enough for a single generation of Americans to pay off our debt. Unless our productivity and output grows, the Treasury projects that within a generation the federal debt will rise to 100 percent of GDP, as our future commitments come due, and suddenly become part of the nation's acknowledged debt.

This will have a devastating financial impact on the nation. Balancing the federal budget will not be nearly enough, as economists document. The federal government would have to run a substantial surplus continuously for 75 years just to prevent the debt to GDP ratio from rising.

---

12 http://newamerica.net/publications/articles/2013/a_new_us_grand_strategy_77134

PRODUCTIVITY GROWTH, ANNUAL PERCENTAGE
1890-2006[13]

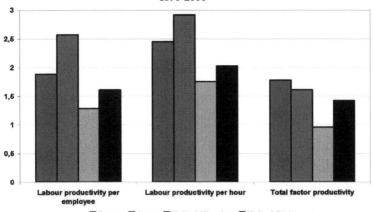

■ France ■ Japan □ United Kingdom ■ United States

We cannot cut spending enough to erase the debt. If interest rates rise, then overnight we could find ourselves unable to even *service* the debt.[14] We can't expand oil and gas drilling enough to erase the deficit. We cannot print money to erase the deficit. To just spend and deplete either our economic or ecological resources are false panaceas, reruns of programming developed to contain a different kind of crisis in a different era. Our only responsible choice is to innovate, and drive improvements of productivity that can overcome economic, social and environmental debts at once.

The second challenge is the Contained Depression.[15] The United States is not experiencing a mere business-cycle

---

13 Gilbert Cette, Yusuf Kocoglu, Jacques Mairesse, "A comparison of productivity in France, Japan, the United Kingdom and the United States over the past century," Banque de France, 2008

14 David Stockman, speaking at the Future 500 UnConvention, at the Commit Forum, 2012, see http://www.youtube.com/watch?v=q1ngI0FxLxY

15 Patrick Doherty, New America Foundation, A New U.S. Grand Strategy, see http://newamerica.net/publications/articles/2013/a_new_us_grand_strategy_77134

downturn—this is a "contained depression," as Patrick Doherty of New America Foundation writes in *Foreign Policy*.[16] The 2008 financial crisis triggered a broad deleveraging, a debt crisis that spanned across households and businesses. Incomes failed to service record levels of consumer and corporate debt, further reducing employment and in turn reducing revenues to state and federal governments.

While Federal Reserve policy, the TARP bailout, and the stimulus bill may have contained the worst of the short-term economic pain, the limits of monetary policy are in sight. The federal funds rate is effectively zero; quantitative easing is merely propping up asset prices to contain unemployment; and former Fed Chairman Ben Bernanke's "maturity extension program" has now expired, after trading $667 billion in short-term securities for longer-term notes. Meanwhile, American households and businesses have only begun to address their deep indebtedness.

The Federal Reserve can no longer generate the circumstances necessary to end the underlying depression—reviving aggregate demand and restoring the economics of lending and equity investment. Keynesian stimulus may make sense when the economy is operating below capacity. But when innovation, not consumption, is called for, further debt simply represents a caffeine-powered jolt to status quo. It fails to nourish the creative resources that now need to be brought to the fore, to create new value.

Congress can't act either, and wouldn't choose to, even if it could overcome gridlock. Pumping more stimulus dollars into the economy or fixing the federal debt won't lead to innovation. Consumer preferences have shifted such that pumping more money into fixing old infrastructure or directly into citizens'

---

16 *Ibid.*

30

bank accounts will have no lasting effect beyond propping up the old, unsustainable economy and adding to deficits. In the short and medium terms, borrowing rates for the U.S. government will remain low and will not crowd out private lending, meaning the extraordinary amount of political attention being paid to long-term entitlements is only partly justified. Cutting entitlements alone is no solution; cutting them too quickly or severely could make matters worse.

Well before the country hits the entitlement wall, the economy is at great risk of deepening its austerity spiral as businesses shed employees to appear more profitable to shareholders. That will further reduce household incomes, decreasing demand and government revenue in turn. Meanwhile, extended American economic weakness will only exacerbate the global macroeconomic risk from the Eurozone to China.

The third global business challenge is the Resilience Deficit.[17] The systems, supply chains, and infrastructure that connect our markets are fragile and prone to disruption. Today's "value chains" are designed to increase efficiency but have little redundancy. This places a business premium on stasis. Maintaining constant trend lines, reinforcing existing power relationships, and insulating against innovation, becomes increasingly important to protecting existing assets. Consider the March 2011 Japanese tsunami, for instance: this natural disaster curtailed production of auto parts used by all six major American and Japanese automakers, shutting down production plants across the United States and helping to drive up unemployment from 8.9 to 9.1 percent. In October 2011, flooding in Thailand led to global disruptions in U.S. computer manufacturing. Around the same time, China shut off exports of

---

17 *Ibid.*

rare-earth minerals—it produces 95 percent of the global supply—for three months. As a result, prices for light bulbs, wind turbines, and batteries spiked.

The economic risk of zero resilience is akin to the effects of turning a complex natural rainforest into a single-crop monoculture. Single-commodity production may be maximized, but only as long as there is no change in climate or circumstances. Then, the single commodity for which the system has been optimized may suddenly face total collapse.

Zero resilience also limits the capacity to invest in infrastructure renewal. With margins stretched to the limit, the incentive is to rely on increasingly overstretched infrastructures, since competition discourages individual economic actors from investing in renewal. It's not just supply chains. Infrastructure arrears in the United States alone stand at $2.2 trillion. And that is just to get the bridges, roads, railways, schools, ports, and airports that undergird the Cold War-era economic engine up to standard. Little thought is given to cultivating a 21st century infrastructure that takes full advantage of the productivity-enhancing potential of information technologies.

Consequences are many and varied. America's food system periodically spreads E. coli and other pathogens across the country. And in 2008, we watched as toxic mortgage-backed assets from the American market spread globally, contributing to disruptions from the Royal Bank of Scotland to the Greek treasury.

The fourth of these challenges is Economic Inclusion.[18] The ranks of the world's nouveau riche are swelling. The planet is on track to welcome three billion new members of the global middle class in the next 20 years. For those fortunate enough to

---

18 *Ibid.*

climb out of poverty, advancement today translates into a 300 percent increase in income, but also a 300 percent increase in resource consumption.

The enhanced income is desirable for each individual, but without a major improvement in resource productivity, the three-fold multiplier in consumption will strain global supplies of clean air and pure water, overharvest fisheries, and degrade the quality of natural systems like the oceans, forests, and atmosphere. We are simply not able to meet the needs of this new middle class unless we can expand the productivity of energy and raw materials, to deliver more value for any level of consumption. Over the last 20 years, the world absorbed just one billion new consumers, sending commodity prices up more than 300 percent in the past decade. Prices are poised for further gains, and we know that when the prices of strategic commodities rise sufficiently, markets do not adapt so much as states intervene to gain or preserve access to them, whether energy, water, food, or strategic minerals.

The fifth global business challenge is Ecosystem Depletion.[19] Civilization relies on a healthy global ecosystem to provide the air, water, and land-based resources that support life. It is important that we live within the budget nature provides—the extraordinary creative output of the planet's biosystems. When we begin to consume the systems themselves, we reduce the earth's capacity to support us later.

Over the past century, human activity has grown so vast that we have begin to disrupt the equilibrium of the Earth's planetary systems. We are emitting too much carbon, changing the chemistry of both freshwater and saltwater bodies, and overconsuming the natural capital we rely on to produce life-giving ecosystem services.

---

19 *Ibid.*

These ecological debts cannot long be concealed with policies that insulate us from their effects. Rising acidity in the world's oceans—a consequence of increasing atmospheric CO_2, 30-40 percent of which is absorbed into the sea—dramatically reduces the ocean's capacity to provide for our increasing protein needs. Industrial activity has already increased ocean acidity 30 percent, as measured by H+ ion concentration, and the rate of change is increasing.[20] Since two-thirds of new protein is expected to come from the oceans,[21] this change in pH level threatens our capacity to feed ourselves, and places hundreds of millions of lives at risk.

The conversion of the planet's rainforests, home to more than two-thirds of the world's genetic biological diversity, undermines both the productivity and resilience of the forests. During the past 40 years, for example, close to 20 percent of the Amazon rainforest has been clearcut—more than in the previous 450 years since the start of European colonization. Soon, the forest's ecology could begin to unravel. An intact rainforest produces half its own rainfall through the moisture it releases into the atmosphere. Reduce that through clearing, and the remaining trees dry out and die. That reduces river levels, which can lead to disasters like those that left hundreds of Brazilian Amazon communities without water in 2005.[22]

These threats to air, water, and land-based ecosystems are in addition to the risks of climate change caused by ever-increasing burning of fossil fuels. Fearing excessive command-and-control of the economy, a significant part of the political right has chosen to

---

20 Orr, James C.; et al. (2005). "Anthropogenic ocean acidification over the twenty-first century and its impact on calcifying organisms". Nature 437 (7059): 681–686. Bibcode:2005Natur.437..681O. doi:10.1038/nature04095. PMID 16193043. Archived from the original on 2008-06-25. Cite uses deprecated parameters (help)

21 http://www.un.org/en/sustainablefuture/oceans.shtml

22 http://environment.nationalgeographic.com/environment/habitats/last-of-amazon/

evade the issue of climate change, pretending that the science of climate has no basis, or that the actions required would so limit our freedoms that changing temperatures and sea levels are a worthwhile sacrifice. But this head-in-the-sands approach can ultimately lead to the consequence the Right most firmly wishes to avoid: global restraints on economic growth imposed by government responding to a crisis, where we no longer have the capacity to make sound long-term decisions.

Part of the Left has taken the opposite course, sounding alarms so loud and long that no one can hear them, and oversimplifying the science in an attempt to make it seem more exacting than it is. Climate activists are right that the risks are real. But they are wrong when they convey that they precisely know what those risks are, at various levels of CO_2 concentration. And they are misguided when they deny the legitimacy of the worries of the Right, or seek to bury them in alarmism. A Left-only path to climate protection will go nowhere, political or environmentally. Only Right and Left together, with both their purposes advanced, can protect the planet.

The business community and conservative political forces hold the key to sensible environmental protection policy. They choose obstruction only at their peril. Their better approach is to provide the margin for political victory; if they choose action over inaction, they can set the logical terms by which we reduce environmental risk while protecting individual freedom and economic vitality. If they wait, they will be forced to accept an agenda in which centralized government control is the driving force.

Shirking this responsibility would come at a great cost, perhaps the greatest cost. With no further change in policy, we will see our oceans and forests decline, our air and water contaminated, and as much as a 6-degree Celsius warming by the end of the century. Well before 2050, we could face widespread food insecurity, economic disruption, mass human migration, and regional war as these critical systems degrade.

These five challenges—debt, depression, resilience, inclusion, and depletion—will determine both the economic performance and geopolitical threats of the coming decades. Worse, they are interdependent: we cannot accommodate three billion new consumers without addressing ocean health, climate change, America's austerity spiral, or the design of the country's outmoded infrastructure. It is, as the engineers say, a wicked problem. Yet, large though it is, America has a tool for addressing this scale of challenge.

A NEW GRAND STRATEGY

Harness Creativity, Diversity
and Entrepreneurship

As Patrick Doherty writes in the January 2013 *Foreign Policy*, a grand strategy for the United States is a generation's commitment to create the conditions necessary for the country to pursue the great purposes set forth in the preamble of the U.S. Constitution. It looks at the world, it looks at America, and it defines the broad path the country must take to advance its most sacred objectives.[23]

In a grand strategy, principles are more important than plans, and resilience is more desirable than efficiency. The need is not for a rigid command-and-control "plan" that reinforces the status quo and restricts freedom and change, but for natural market-based systems of feedback-and-adaptation that assure that genuine costs are recognized, not concealed, so that innovation is encouraged and supported.

This is an important distinction. Because the 20th century mode of industrial production itself thrived on big institutions with top-down command-and-control management tactics, there is a tendency to follow this same pattern in proposing ways to undo outdated industrial practices.

---

23 *Op. cit.*

37

For example, among some left-of-center environmental activists, there is often a preference for centralized government planning that would lead to a global economic monoculture that reflects a western middle-class view of what a sustainable society should look like.

But consider how it sounds to conservatives when one leading environmental advocate issued a call-to-arms for a government-led solution. Here is how she summarizes her plan:

"Responding to climate change requires that we break every rule in the free-market playbook and that we do so with great urgency. We will need to rebuild the public sphere, reverse privatizations, relocalize large parts of economies, scale back overconsumption, bring back long-term planning, heavily regulate and tax corporations, maybe even nationalize some of them, cut military spending and recognize our debts to the global South. Of course, none of this has a hope in hell of happening unless it is accompanied by a massive, broad-based effort to radically reduce the influence that corporations have over the political process. That means, at a minimum, publicly funded elections and stripping corporations of their status as "people" under the law. In short, climate change supercharges the pre-existing case for virtually every progressive demand on the books, binding them into a coherent agenda based on a clear scientific imperative." [24]

From a progressive U.S.-centric perspective, maybe this vision sounds appealing. But the outcome she envisions would not come into being through the command-and-control methods she proposes. Her approach is akin to building a rainforest, using timber from Home Depot. Her "progressive" prescriptions are a mechanistic compilation of best hits from the early 1970s. There is nothing organic about them—they are forced, urgent, and panicked. They show little understanding of

24 Naomi Klein, Capitalism vs. the Climate, The Nation, Nov. 28, 2011. See http://www.thenation.com/article/164497/capitalism-vs-climate

how sustainability actually works in nature or the economy. And if adopted in whole, they would lock into place a consumptive western-centric lifestyle that would drive more depletion, not less.

This advocate's prescription is remarkably similar to the views expressed by leading "climate skeptics," who genuinely believe that responding to climate change requires that we abandon free markets. The author even attributes some of her insights to opinions they expressed to her. "The deniers did not decide that climate change is a left-wing conspiracy by uncovering some covert socialist plot. They arrived at this analysis by taking a hard look at what it would take to lower global emissions as drastically and as rapidly as climate science demands. They have concluded that this can be done only by radically reordering our economic and political systems in ways antithetical to their 'free market' belief system."

What this advocate has really done is to take a rigidly dogmatic prescription, framed by her ideological adversaries, and conveyed it directly to her followers. It "sells" because it is simplistic, devoid of complex thought and confusing nuance. Fundamentalists on the Left can easily be motivated to cheer it, and on the Right to fear it. Each side can use it to build their political army. Each side believes they are advancing their troops. Each side constructs a solid wall of opposition to any progress whatsoever, locking in policies that erode both freedom and sustainability.

Neither excessive government control nor hands-off policy are likely to happen in the real world. The greater danger we face is that by further deadlocking our gridlocked political system, followers of both extremes will together damage a significant part of both the economy and the ecosystem. And each, having brought about this calamity, will blame the other, and be blind to their own role.

In one respect, as we indicated earlier, we are deep in debt, but we cannot pay off our debt by extracting it from the poor, the middle class, or the environment. The real answer is not to wait for big institutions to impose top-down solutions. It is to empower people to create them, from the bottom up.

AMERICA'S PROMISE

Freedom, Creativity, and Resilience

America's promise is not to drive consumption, or even prosperity. For nearly two-and-a-half centuries, America has championed the creative capacity and entrepreneurial energy of the human spirit. America's prosperity is not our mission—it is a consequence of our mission. Our goal is not to consume value—it is to unleash the capacity of people to create it.

At our best, America is more than a nation—it is a set of ideals to unleash the creative capacities of ever-widening circles of people, inspiring new generations in nations around the world to aspire to the levels of freedom and prosperity that we today enjoy. Even during episodes when our government, business, labor, and other institutions have violated these ideals, our people, given time, have always championed them.

America proves that when people are allowed to express themselves and their capacities freely, they are strong and powerful. Only when our freedoms are repressed—through slavery, prejudice, institutional barriers, conformity, or dependency—they can be held back.

Last century's prosperity benefited almost all Americans, but it also came at a price. The focus on production and consumption favored top-down systems of economic and political regulation that advantaged sets of qualities and skills. Men secured more power than women in this formulation; engineering and science were more valued than art and beauty;

conformity was cheaper than diversity; factory and office labor was often better compensated than crafts, artistry, and distinctive forms of creativity.

But we no longer live in a primarily mass manufacturing economy. Huge generic top-down institutions are increasingly out-performed by smaller, smarter, more decentralized organizations where initiative is democratized and people are valued in all their diverse forms. The economy is not so much like a jungle any more, where like individuals compete and only the strongest survive. It is more like a rainforest, a complex system where diversity is the norm, in which it's not the survival of the fittest—it's the survival of all who fit. Almost everyone in the emerging economy can find their place. When given the freedom to be themselves, to make their distinctive contributions, there is nothing weak or needy about them. What they need is not dependency—it is opportunity.

Today, America's great challenge is no longer to out-produce the rest of the world. Indeed, production alone, if it represses innovation, sacrifices freedom, and is paid for by economic or ecological debt, is not a sustainable source of livelihood for two, three, four or more billion people living on a small planet. Rather, the great global project, for America and all the world's developed nations, is to create ever more value for more people, using fewer resources and creating less pollution and waste.

Ending decentralized free markets in favor of central control—whether following an old-left or old-right archetype—would only drive debts higher. Neither a corporate-dominated "productive" global factory run on fossil fuels, nor a government-dominated "sustainable" variation of American suburb is a viable path to a resilient, sustainable economy.

The course that is more likely to succeed is one that unleashes the creative capacity of individuals and communities to adapt at the local level to new global realities. It is a path that favors small business over big, local control over central control, innovation over consumption, genuine diversity over think-alike conformity. It emulates complex adaptive systems like rainforests, not simplistic centrally-designed monocultures like those we grew dependent on in the last era.

Disruptive forces are already upending traditional business models, cultural norms, and political alliances. These can help bring into being a new economy that is dynamic, resilient, adaptive, diversified, sustainable and prosperous. It is not the virtue of business that causes it to adapt, but the imperatives of the marketplace, as new ideas and technologies displace old ones.

But American politics is lagging. It faces few imperatives to adapt; its bias favors yesterday's interests, who are clearly defined are well-represented, not tomorrow's, who are not exactly known and almost never organized.

Stuck in battles of the mid-20th century, both major parties spend too much effort appeasing vested interests. This is understandable—we all have vested interests we want to protect, whether it is the interests of rich, middle or poor; men or women; gay or straight; senior, middle or young.

But when it comes to a healthy future, those interests are not fundamentally at odds. We will each do poorly if the systems that sustain us are unhealthy. We can each do well if those systems are robust and resilient.

To meet the global challenges of World War II and the Cold War, America's grand strategy as practiced by Presidents Franklin D. Roosevelt, Harry Truman, and Dwight Eisenhower aligned three great levers of power: the nation's economic engine, its foreign policy, and its governing institutions.

In both World War II and the Cold War, the secret to America's success was that the country harnessed its economy to do the heavy lifting. In World War II, America became the Arsenal of Democracy, outproducing the Axis. The country enlisted its industry to arm and equip its allies while building up its own military from 450,000 troops to 16 million; it aggressively pursued the war aims enshrined in the Atlantic Charter; and it reorganized government to enable it to pursue both aims. In the Cold War, America could not defeat the Soviets militarily, so it organized a system of containment to best them in a longer-term contest of economic and political systems.[25]

And best them America did. To ensure the Soviets' defeat, Truman and Eisenhower established a framework of taxes, codes, and spending policies that helped drive suburban housing, consumer goods production, and reconstruction materials for Europe and Japan. By the time candidates John F. Kennedy and Richard Nixon debated in 1960, the strategy had fused with America's cultural DNA—it was fully adopted and internalized by both political parties, corporate leadership, government bureaucracy, and the American people. Since the Soviet Union's 1991 collapse, however, the United States has failed to identify, adopt, or implement a revised grand strategy.

Instead, over the past 20 years, the United States' default strategy has been to incrementally adjust national security and economic policies to defend and extend its Cold War economic engine. The result is the unsustainable U.S. and international order. Walking backwards does not lead us to the future. The productivity revolution of the last era opens a path to a future of cleaner energy, limited government, human-scale enterprise, more prosperity, and greater freedom.

---

25 *Op. cit.*

THE FIRST PRODUCTIVITY
REVOLUTION

The Triumph of Prosperity in America

America's political and economic paralysis follows closely on one of our greatest historic triumphs: unprecedented material prosperity. Before World War II, in all prior civilizations and social orders, "the vast bulk of humanity had been preoccupied with responding to basic material needs," writes Brink Lindsey. "Postwar America, however, was different. An extensive and highly complex division of labor unleashed enormous productive powers far beyond anything in prior human experience. As a result, the age-old bonds of scarcity were broken. Concern with physical survival and security was now banished to the periphery of social life."

America's triumph was built on the radical increase in labor productivity brought about by industrialization. Between 1890 and 1990, U.S. labor productivity exploded 14-fold. Workers generated 14 times more value per hour at the end than the beginning of the twentieth century. That explosive growth was enabled by three primary drivers.

First, it came from the capacity of machines to take a prototype design and replicate it over and over, to scale production of goods to unprecedented levels and enable a huge middle class to enjoy benefits once available only to the rich.

Second, it came from the methods of scientific management, which broke production processes down into simple, replicable tasks that could be carried out across assembly lines by almost anyone with basic skills.

Third, it came from huge increases in resource consumption. We saved human labor, but we substituted fossil fuels and raw materials.

The first factor, machines, is a source of value that can be sustained over the long run. Machines multiply not just muscle, but also mind. They take a prototype invention, something conceived by human creativity, and replicate it over and over, shaping raw materials into functional designs that deliver real value with increasing returns to scale.

The second factor, simplified work tasks, is also sustainable. It enables a business to hire workers with limited skills and train them to perform production functions over and over. Workers become very small parts in a very large whole. The result is a big paycheck at work, and cheap goods at home.

The third factor, increased resource consumption, is not sustainable. Material resources are inherently limited. We cannot increase consumption indefinitely.

LABOR PRODUCTIVITY GAIN, 1890-1990 (1890 = 1)

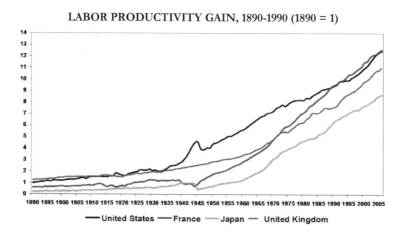

THE ROOT OF THE CONFLICT:

Two Worldviews

The Left's bias to spend economic resources, and the Right's bias to spend energy and environmental resources, come from two distinctly different worldviews that include two very different views on the ultimate source of wealth.

To the conservative mind, nature is often seen as a source of limits, while a free market economy is a source of opportunities. Life in a state of nature is harsh, as 17th Century philosopher Thomas Hobbes famously wrote in *Leviathan*. In order to survive, people must focus primarily on protecting their own self-interest, and that of their family and local community. This can be achieved through a combination of moral and market forces. Moral standards, often codified by religion, motivate people to consider the needs of others, especially their families and neighbors. Market forces harness their self-interest to advance the interest of others.

To the liberal mind, nature is often seen to provide us with the resources we need for life, while a free market exploits those limited resources for selfish, short-term gain. Life in a state of nature is peaceful and sufficient, as Jean-Jacques Rousseau wrote in countering Hobbes. People have all they need, if they take only their share. In the face of this sufficiency, most people will behave selflessly if liberated from societal constraints. They will sacrifice some of their own self-interest to support others, so that others can selflessly give to society. They will "live simply so others may simply live." Western civilization has corrupted this, some on the Left believe. Moral standards and imposed shortages constrain people from simply being themselves, and doing what is best for others. Market forces compel them to stifle their generosity, and consume in such vast quantities that they deplete the resources that others need. These forces undermine our humanity and threaten to deplete the natural resources that sustain us, some believe.

Both the Right and Left hold part of the truth. Nature is a source of limits and opportunities. People are both selfish and selfless. Moral standards are sometimes necessary, and sometimes limiting. Markets both create value, and exploit nature. A system that carries one or the other of these ideologies to an extreme cannot continue to thrive.

The Right is correct in sensing the extraordinary capacity of free markets to create value. Many on the Right recognize that the economy is a complex living system that creates value through the dynamic interplay of people, organizations, and resources. They are aghast at how readily the Left leaps at the opportunity to regulate this vital system. They know that when you dam it, plug it up and seek to control it excessively, you can destroy its creative capacity.

The Left is correct in sensing the extraordinary threat to the ability of nature to sustain economies and societies. Many on the Left recognize that nature is a complex living system that creates value through the dynamic interplay of organisms, communities, and resources. They are aghast at how readily the Right leaps at the opportunity to drill through the heart of this vital system. They know that when you dam it, plug it up, and seek to control it excessively, you can destroy its capacity to sustain human life and support human enterprises.

These two very different worldviews appreciate different aspects of value creation. One values nature, the other values the human economy. But nature and the human economy are interdependent. Right and Left both see parts of the same whole system—the system of human activity in nature, a system with feedback-and-adaptation that creates all value, and sustains all life. The Right sees the economic part of this system. The Left sees the ecological part of this system. The Right reminds us that, from a fiscal perspective, we are running out of money and deep in debt. We cannot continue to grow the economy by borrowing or printing more money. The Left reminds us that, ecologically, we are running out of nature and deep in debt. "Drill baby drill" is just another form of exploitive deficit spending. We cannot continue to grow the economy by depleting the earth.

If we provide the right incentives, Right and Left will begin to recognize that they are seeing parts of the same system. And they will discover that the same policies that cultivate innovation in the economy can also protect and restore a healthy natural environment.

Most Americans believe there is truth on both sides. A nation of innovators reflects the sensibilities of these Americans, regardless of whether they lean right or lean left, and brings them together.

REVOLUTION AND EVOLUTION

Three Forces of Change

*"The number one benefit of information technology
is that it empowers people to do what they want to do.
It lets people be creative. It lets people be productive.
It lets people learn things they didn't think they could
learn before and so in a sense it is all about potential."*

– Steve Ballmer, former Microsoft CEO

We live in a time of change. Three forces are transforming our world: the decline of industrialism as the driving force of the global economy, the rise of information and telecommunications as the new chief catalyst for growth, and the spread of globalization, connecting every nation, community, and individual to every other, and linking together their fates in ways that we cannot easily predict.

These changes are part revolutionary, and part evolutionary. They are revolutionary in that, very often, they disrupt long-dominant legal and cultural institutions. They are evolutionary in that incremental change is accelerated. Qualities like size, strength, and uniformity become less valuable and speed, adaptability, resilience become more so.

If trends continue, this century will see rapid movement along this path. According to futurist John Peterson of the

Arlington Institute, the change could be 1000-fold greater than in the last century. Think about that. The last century began with horse buggies, a national post office, and dynamite. It ended with the Internet, airplanes, email, and weapons too horrific to use. Almost everything was transformed in the process, from factories and farms to families, communities, and nations.

How will the century ahead end? If the pace of change is 70 times as fast, how different will our lives be, in the year 2100? Discontinuous change is almost a certainty. Our lives could be radically different by the next turning.

That change will be for the better and for the worse. It will create risk. It will create opportunity. The net effect—whether we move forward or back overall—depends on how skillfully we adapt to unpredictable, uncontrollable, unprecedented change.

Ideologues on the Left and Right will resist this change. Each holds a fixed view of what society should look like, often looking to the past to project the future. Each seeks to use government, corporate, or religious power to forcibly shape the world, and the people and businesses within it, to fit their preconceptions.

But America's future will not fit into any utopian straightjacket. God and nature have different plans for us, and if we are wise, our future will reflect the varied choices of a diverse and free people who do not fear change, but embrace it.

PROGRAMS WIN ELECTIONS, BUT SYSTEMS BRING SOLUTIONS

Two Systems that Drive Innovation and Create Value

Pro·gram (prō-gram) *noun* – a process carried out according to fixed instructions for the automatic performance of a particular task.

Sys·tem (sis-təm) *noun* – a set of connected parts working together as a complex adaptive unitary whole.

Politicians love programs. Programs win elections. If people are out of work, programs give them jobs. If they are hungry, programs give them food. If they are poor, programs give them money.

Programs enable politicians to deliver specific results to constituents they want to serve. Programs are "proof points" they use to convince voters and contributors they are doing their jobs.

Republicans, whose worldview generally suggests that people will be selfish unless disciplined, like programs that discipline people. They spend tax dollars on police to fight crime, on the military to fight wars, and on border patrols to keep out illegal immigrants seeking a better life in a better system.

Democrats, whose worldview sometimes suggests that everyday people will be selfless if liberated from all constraints, like programs that support people. They spend tax dollars on jobs programs to increase employment, on food programs to feed the hungry, and on aid programs to alleviate poverty, regardless of the effectiveness or beneficiaries.

These programs may be necessary, at least temporarily. But the assumptions underlying them—whether on the Right or on the Left—are not always accurate. People are a mix of selfish and selfless. Our policies, programs, and systems need to reflect that.

Programs cost money, and it is increasingly difficult to find money to pay for the all-you-can-eat buffet of programs we might like, especially as they accumulate over the years. We need to limit the accumulation of programs, and even reduce their number and size. Instead, we need systems that drive prosperity across many measures, by empowering and rewarding people to create value.

Systems are different from programs, in three important ways. First, systems are wholes—interconnected parts working together as a complex adaptive unitary whole. Programs are parts or sets of parts that operate according to fixed rules without adapting. Second, systems have emergent qualities; they create value. Programs have no emergent qualities; they consume resources to do their work. Third, systems always pay for programs—they are the source of net gain that enables programs to function.

Every system has qualities that are absent in its parts. These qualities are sources of new net value. When atoms and molecules join together in a cell, new value emerges: life. When cells join together in a human body, new value emerges: thought, consciousness, and everything that follows.

In society, when people come together to meet their individual and collective needs, new value emerges: families, communities, businesses, economies, nations, civilizations. Each part in these systems imposes net costs. Those costs can only be sustained because, together, the emergent qualities and their net value make the whole system sustainable—even after taking the costs of resources and pollution into account.

Parts in isolation have no way to pay for themselves. They lack the exchanges with a larger environment, the emergent qualities, the net value creation. Programs can only be paid for if they are part of larger systems that generate sustainable net value.

Programs are often necessary to meet essential needs. Often, they are essential parts of larger systems. But programs cannot be paid for without systems. So we need systems that are able to maintain themselves and pay for whatever programs we decide to keep.

The two systems that pay for all programs—in fact, the two systems that pay for everything—are the economy and the ecosystem. These two are the root source of all prosperity. But when our policies seek to sacrifice one of these for the other, they undermine our prosperity, which depends on both. Rather than following the prescription of either the Right or the Left, to drill or spend our way to ruin, we need to draw on the combined wisdom of both the Right and the Left and harness the capacity of these two systems to create value.

Our economic and ecological systems both drive innovation and create value through complex processes of feedback and adaptation. Both suffer decline when we artificially interfere with feedback that drives innovation and creates value. And both currently suffer from major breaks in the flow of feedback.

These breaks take the form of two massive subsidies, enshrined by government and supported by vested economic interests. These subsidies artificially repress essential feedback and retard genuine growth by concealing key costs of doing business. When that happens, costs rise and begin to spin out of control.

The economic subsidies come in the form of massive government spending, dangerous levels of borrowing from other countries, and exponentially growing deficits. These subsidies are championed by the Left, rationalized by vested interests, and supported by demonizers and deniers who pretend that economic limits are not real.

The ecological subsidies come in the form of massive environmental exploitation, pollution, depletion, and degradation. These subsidies are championed by the Right, rationalized by vested interests, and supported by demonizers and deniers who pretend that ecological limits are not real.

Through this massive double-dose of deficit spending, America is burying its children in both economic and ecological debt.

When we recklessly spend either economic or environmental resources, we subsidize activities that erode our prosperity. We support old business and governmental processes that need to change. We freeze jobs and companies in old forms that need to be brought up to date. We create the illusion of well-being, and pretend that the cost is unrelated to it. We retard innovations that could create genuine prosperity.

It is time to stop spending down our prosperity, and learn to replenish it. Living within our means will not be so difficult as we imagine. In fact, it is the surest way to increase our prosperity. Every good parent knows this, and cultivates it in their children. The benefits will be beyond anything we can yet fully conceive, because they will be delivered by an invisible hand with a green thumb.

Fundamentally, the answer is not to add expensive new programs, or tough new regulations, mandates, commands, or controls. Our first priority should be to ensure that the overarching system is designed to maximize sustainable value.

Here is one way.

THE INNOVATION NATION

Toward a Second Productivity Revolution

Stop Growing Debt. Create Value.

Stop Blocking Creativity. Cultivate Entrepreneurism.

Stop Taxing Prosperity. Tax Pollution.

Stop Subsidizing the Past. Invent the Future.

Stop Sowing Dependency. Foster Empowerment.

Stop Empowering Big Government and Corporations.
Empower People.

"Innovation distinguishes a leader from a follower."

– Steve Jobs

In February 2011, the respected McKinsey Global Institute issued a stark report, *Growth and Renewal in the United States: Retooling America's Economic Engine.* Their machine-age metaphor may have been misplaced, but their conclusion was right on target. If the U.S. cannot boost productivity growth rates by a third, the consequences will be painful, and far more damaging to U.S. prosperity than a double-dip into the Great Recession.

"More than ever, the United States needs productivity gains to drive growth and competitiveness," the McKinsey team wrote. "This acceleration needs to come both from efficiency gains—reducing inputs for given output—and from increasing the volume and value of outputs for any given input."

Labor productivity gains alone are not enough, McKinsey wrote. It is important that the United States return to the "broadly-based productivity growth of the 1990s when strong demand and a shift to products with a higher value per unit helped to create jobs even as productivity was growing."

In short, the U.S. needs to begin to replicate last century's 14-fold leap in productivity. But this time, higher value per unit will be less about labor productivity and more about resource and energy productivity. These new productivity factors will determine whether we achieve anything close to the gains of the last century.

Such leaps in resource and energy productivity are within reach, but they are not assured. As globalization and technology connect and speed up the world, they create the potential for new breakdowns, in which we succumb to economic or ecological limits. They also create the potential for new breakthroughs, in which we transcend yesterday's limits and achieve both economic prosperity and environmental sustainability.

Creative people—and the technologies they invent—can birth a second revolution in productivity, in which we no longer need to trade ecological assets for economic ones. The combination of the microchip, computers, the Internet, advanced materials, advanced recycling, renewable energy, clean technologies and other innovations on the horizon can increase the amount of wealth we create per unit of energy by more than tenfold by the end of this century.

The actions of creative people will inevitably disrupt the traditional roles of big corporations and big government, but this is healthy for them as well as us. Those institutions are instruments designed to serve people, not the other way around. The philosophy they should live by is the one retailer Home Depot grew its business on: "You can do it. We can help." People create value. We need help from businesses and governments to help.

Among the deliverables we need and expect from our businesses and government are simple incentives—feedback systems to drive up prosperity and environmental sustainability, and drive down the consumption and cost of fossil fuel dependence. Sometimes, establishing those systems requires mandates. But mandates often have unintended consequences and create bad incentives. Sometimes, they can be established by voluntary actions, such as by harnessing the buying power of people and companies in the free market. But reliance on voluntary actions often allows free riders to benefit without paying their share. However, there is a third option—common sense incentives that require consumers and businesses to pay for the full costs of resources they use and pollution they impose, and give them reasons to invest in improvements in resource and energy productivity.

TEN PRINCIPLES OF AN INNOVATION NATION

Empower People to Create Value

1. SET A NATIONAL GOAL. Target a 3 percent annual gain in overall productivity in public policy, not as a singular mandate, but as a target to guide our progress.

2. SET SECTOR GOALS. Leading companies in each sector set their own goals, in consultation with experts and stakeholders, that support 3 percent national gain.

3. UNLEASH PEOPLE. Cut barriers to individual enterprise, both public and private.

4. REFORM TAXES. Stop taxing jobs, growth, and prosperity—tax pollution instead.

5. WIND DOWN SUBSIDIES. Stop subsidizing the past—wean us off unnecessary spending.

6. INCREASE RESEARCH. Fund R&D for the future, to drive resource breakthroughs.

7. PROTECT AIR, WATER, AND LAND. Reduce environmental and climate risks, and use the market to foster conservation and stewardship.

8. RENEW CITIES AND COMMUNITIES. Reform outdated codes and end barriers to the sharing economy to revitalize big cities, small towns, and local communities.

9. REFORM GOVERNANCE. Move beyond gridlock, toward government that is democratic, functional, and free.

10. INCLUDE EVERYONE. Celebrate the capacities of all people in all their diversity, respecting and welcoming women and men, gay and straight, minorities and majorities to contribute fully, without prejudice.

1

SET A NATIONAL GOAL

Target a 3 percent annual gain in overall productivity in public policy, not as a singular mandate, but as a target to guide our progress.

Business leaders in collaboration with stakeholders from across civil society need to target a national goal: a 3 percent annual gain in overall productivity, combining actions in the marketplace, research and development, and policy advocacy. This 3 percent solution can double prosperity and halve pollution and consumption every 25 years. It can drive a fourfold prosperity gain in a half-century, and more than ten-fold by 2100, while cutting pollution and carbon intensity 75 to 90 percent or more. The payoffs to business and stakeholders include more jobs, better pay, healthy profits, expanded use of information technology, modernized manufacturing and agriculture, wider opportunities for entrepreneurship, and enhanced lifestyle choices.

Many companies already embrace a 3 percent or similar goal. Coca-Cola, Intel, CSX, Dell, Sprint Nextel, Kohl's, MFS, Avon, Best Buy, Brown-Forman, Legg Mason, Norfolk Southern, Raytheon, Stanley Black & Decker, and McKinsey & Company are among those who collaborated to develop "The 3% Solution," an initiative with the World Wildlife Fund (WWF).[26]

---

26 https://worldwildlife.org/projects/the-3-solution

The 3% Solution focuses on increasing productivity as measured by carbon intensity, an energy metric that favors lowering carbon emissions. But the environmental and health benefits are broader. From a natural resources perspective, increased productivity combined with policies that internalize externalities can alleviate potential shortages of water, energy, minerals, and food. A 3 percent annual productivity gain doubles the effective years-remaining of limited resources every 24 years, enabling sustainable consumption levels that keep supplies from being exhausted.

Government will not lead an effort for a 3 percent solution. But it will support and advance it, if corporate and civic stakeholders step forward first. Business leaders must do so, not just in the public interest but in their own interest.

That will require an enhanced approach to corporate government affairs. In the old economy, where growth and change tended to follow predictable linear patterns, the function of corporate lobbying was often to either veto change, or shape it to reinforce status quo interests.

This led companies to take a narrow and short-sighted approach to public policy. Government affairs was carried out through generic policy intermediaries such as trade associations, chambers of commerce, and K-Street government affairs units, whose stock-in-trade often involves protecting existing business practices and power arrangements by vetoing policy innovation. These professionals could secure and protect narrow tax and regulatory benefits specific to their clients. But they were discouraged from taking a broader approach to policy, where multiple stakeholder interests might be better served. Any such public-spirited adventures inevitably involved controversy, and lobbyists discouraged their clients from "using their chits" in these Quixotic pursuits.

Companies cannot be expected to sacrifice their short-term survival interests for broader public interests. But it is their responsibility and our expectation that they will serve interests bigger than just themselves, and help shape policies so private and public interests are mutually reinforcing. This is not optional. It is part of every company's social license to operate. Supporting a robust and prosperous community is ultimately in the best interest of every company.

In addition to the companies above, many others are taking a higher-level approach to public policy. Walmart, Nestle, Unilever, Coca-Cola, and almost 50 other brands work collaboratively through the Consumer Goods Forum to improve social and environmental performance across their supply chains.

But so far, these initiatives are in their infancy. They sometimes still avoid policy related work, deeming this beyond their scope. When policy positions do emerge from these initiatives, they lack an institution that can bring them forward to political leaders. Trade groups and chambers of commerce, as important as they are, cannot effectively do this work while effectively covering the short-term interests of companies.

Traditional government affairs organizations protect important interests, but they tend to err toward the interests of the past, not the future. Their job is to eliminate barriers to existing patterns of consumption and debt-creation, not to foster genuine innovation and value-creation. They tend to empower large centralized institutions, not the individuals and small enterprises that are the wellspring of value creation.

The political class is simply doing its job. Gridlock and deadlock are better than innovation and adaptation, in protecting short-term interests. It also ensures that they keep their jobs. Neither lawmakers nor lobbyists will be able to lead.

But they can support and advance the future, if their work is used to support systemic change that serves society as a whole. C-suite business leaders can only serve their shareholders and stakeholders if they collaborate to advance an innovative, resilient, and increasingly resource-productive economy within which enterprise as a whole can excel.

2

SET SECTOR GOALS

Leading companies in each sector set their own goals, in consultation with experts and stakeholders that support 3% national gain.

Technology companies working collaboratively have identified ways their technologies could promote growth while cutting U.S. energy use almost 20 percent. Consumer packaged goods (CPG) companies working through the Consumer Goods Forum (CGF) estimate they could save roughly 5 percent of the world's energy just through collaborative change across their supply chains. Imagine what could be accomplished if the leading companies in every sector—transportation, energy, housing, health and more—pursued aggressive goals to improve resource productivity?

Quite possibly, they could improve resource productivity, create value, create jobs, and protect the environment much more effectively than government.

Part of the reason is the power they exert over their supply chains. When Congress sets energy objectives, companies often oppose them. But when a major brand with the buying power of a Walmart or Unilever sets an objective, thousands of suppliers compete to meet the goals. Major brands and retailers have the capacity to drive productivity gains across the economy; and increasingly, they use that power. In response to Congress's request, the lobbyist's answer is often, "we can't do it that soon, if at all." When Walmart asks, the CEO's answer is, "is tomorrow soon enough?"

Another reason private sector goals are more readily met is that they are adaptive. If Unilever's goal really is unrealistic, it will soon learn why, and can adjust accordingly. Laws and regulations are much less adaptive to new information or changing circumstances.

One factor that limits sectoral goal-setting, however, is outdated tax and regulatory frameworks that subsidize consumption and penalize change. The right set of regulatory and tax reforms, some discussed below, would reward companies that harness their market power to improve resource productivity.

In the 20th century economy, while the private sector focused on maximizing production, the public sector established rules and programs to manage externalities like pollution, public health, unemployment, and poverty. Today, business can often accomplish much more than government in reducing these problems as well. For example, when Walmart makes a commitment to offer low-cost prescriptions to millions of customers, or reduce the environmental footprint of its products, it drives change across thousands of suppliers globally, in ways that Congress won't, and probably can't.

Consider forestry, for example. Deforestation accounts for 15 percent of climate change. Four commodities account for about 70 percent of this impact, or over 10 percent of global emissions. If we can downshift 80 percent of the carbon impacts from these, we cut global emissions 8 percent, in one sector alone.[27]

---

27 Interview with Jeff Seabright, Vice President, Energy and Water Resources, The Coca-Cola Company, April 2014

Multiply that by similar efforts in several sectors, and we could potentially achieve 40 or even 50 percent reductions.

Combine those leapfrog changes with the innovation effect—which now reduces carbon intensity 1-2 percent a year but could be increased to 3-4 percent with a price on carbon—and suddenly global reductions of well over 50 percent become feasible. Keeping temperature increases to around 2-degrees Celsius, without a major command-and-control regimen by government, becomes a realistic possibility.

As long as we have a market-based innovation driven economy—as long as business is one of the key wellsprings of prosperity—the only way to address climate change globally is to transform markets. The actions of 100 companies across several sectors can be the action that brings us to the tipping point, and shifts us from an old consumptive economic model to a restorative one that protects the natural systems on which prosperity depends.

Business needs to step up.

3

UNLEASH PEOPLE

Cut barriers to enterprise, both public and private.

In the generations since World War II, regulations became a chief means by which government helped define "regular" procedures for people and companies to follow in carrying out their functions. Clearly-set rules helped create a level playing field for enterprise, so that companies could compete without imposing externalized costs on local communities.

But the form that these early regulations took was decidedly programmatic, not systemic. Even today, most regulations impose rigid and unbending standards on behavior that may not account for the diversity of local conditions. Rather than enforcing bottom-line performance—the goals of the regulations—the rules are enforced to the letter, not the purpose. People have little incentive to do better than regulations requires. In fact, doing so is often unlawful, if the procedures for excellent results differ from those for good or poor results.

In addition, regulations create market conditions that favor established interests, who can influence, game or capture the regulatory regime, and use the courts to block more innovative enterprises, minimizing competition and change. The courts generally enforce the letter of the law, and look to regulatory bodies to define its spirit or purpose. But these political bodies are generally subjected to pressure from institutionalized interest groups, who benefit from the old rules. There are strong career risks for lawmakers who advocate more logical or just codes and mandates, since they are serving the interests of the future, not the past, and the future employs no lobbyists and makes no contributions.

Regulations serve important purposes. They can be necessary to set minimum safety and environmental performance levels, providing companies with a level playing field on which to compete. But too often, they end up creating unfair advantages for some and burdens for others. Large companies are often in a better position to both shape and comply with regulations. Small and adaptive businesses often pay a disproportionate share of the costs. According to the Small Business Administration, federal regulatory compliance imposes a $1.75 trillion annual cost on the economy, often hitting small businesses and entrepreneurs most severely. No data accounts for the cost of suburban-era local regulations, but they may be greater.

Federal, state, and local regulations dating from the 1950s helped build the nation's superhighways, hugely productive factories and farms, and suburban housing developments, each serviced by lookalike strip malls, shopping centers, and office complexes that fostered fast generic growth. But this basic framework for a drill-and-spend economy lacked a quality important for long-term resilience: the potential to adapt and diversify to meet evolving needs and service more niche-oriented functions. Chain stores and office complexes could thrive in this atmosphere, but start-ups and small enterprises faced major legal and institutional barriers. Women and minorities, especially those in less affluent communities, could not legally establish enterprises to meet their local needs, leaving food, service, child care, and transit deserts where those services were most needed. Mass transit worked within the densely-populated city centers, but failed when stretched to suburbs where density was too low to support a hub. The "last mile" challenge meant that people often needed to use a car to access a bus or train, placing additional strains on adaptive development.

Today, the economy has changed. The effects of small-scale entrepreneurism are far less negative, and far more positive. Yet local politicians on the Right and Left often err severely on the side of status quo interests, preventing the gradual change that keeps communities vital and alive. People in large cities and suburbs face major barriers when they seek to rent rooms in their homes, even in the face of severe housing shortages. They can't legally establish small enterprises open to the public, even when they could help revitalize a neighborhood. They can't compete with licensed taxi services or public transit, without being taken to court. They can't even provide babysitting services for their neighbors, without reconstructing their property to meet city codes, even if this means placing children in genuine danger due to a lack of affordable care options.

This leaves economic development almost solely in the hands of large developers at the local level, and large corporations at the state and federal level, all of whom have the financial resources to withstand or deal with embedded rules and regulations. Over time, their businesses come to be structured around the rules, with government affairs units dedicated to keeping things the same, even codifying the practices they have mastered.

Endless repetition of postwar growth models, dictated by institutionalized rules and regulations Xerox-copied from city-to-city and state-to-state, with variation often prohibited by federal policy, is the ecological equivalent of forcing a forest to remain a simple monoculture dominated by a single species, rather than enabling it to evolve into a complex rainforest supporting vast creativity and diversity. In such a monoculture, consumption is maximized but the system fails to adapt. It keeps copying itself according to a regulatory program in desperate need of hacking.

The public has a legitimate interest in protecting health and safety. But in a fast-changing world, barriers against adaptation and innovation reduce resilience, and undermine survival chances. Replicating and expanding status quo arrangements beyond their utility leads to rising risks and costs for housing, food, transportation, and education. Reforming regulations so that they serve clearly-defined purposes and reward performance would help stimulate organic solutions to problems that just keep on getting bigger under today's command-and-control regimens.

4

REFORM TAXES

Stop taxing jobs, growth, and prosperity—
tax pollution instead.

Today's system of taxation dates back to World War II, the
New Deal and the Depression, when the national imperative
was to maximize production to win the war, create jobs, and
drive the economy to full consumptive capacity.

In that context, it was administratively simpler to tax things
we wanted—like income, jobs, savings, and profits—than to
impose restrictions on the externalities of commerce, like
consumption, pollution, and waste, which were relatively small
and local at the time. But the failure to penalize these
externalities meant that they grew, until they reached a level
where government stepped in to regulate them. The regulations
may have been "good enough"—they set minimal performance
standards with which all companies had to minimally comply.
But were not systematically reduced, and some now may be
having negative effects on human health and the biosystem.

These levies did what they were intended to do: they raised
money for government and allowed production to increase with
minimal restraints. But they also had a major distorting effect
that continues to this day: they tax prosperity. They discourage
work, thrift, and investment. They subsidize pollution, create
dependence on government regulations, and prevent continuous
improvement in social and environmental performance.

A smarter tax would target the actual consumption of energy and resources, through a broad economy-wide shift from taxing prosperity to taxing pollution and depletion. The purpose of this tax reform would be not just to raise revenue. It would also directly drive innovation, create jobs, promote growth, and reduce pollution while reducing the need for government interventions and programs directed to these ends.

When we tax something that increases over time, like prosperity, then taxes increase with it. But when we tax something that declines over time, like rates of pollution, then taxes decline along with them. As a result, a system that taxes pollution would tend over time to reduce taxes, not increase them. The tax itself would help accelerate this effect. Generally speaking, when we tax something, we get less of it. So as we tax pollution, we will reduce it.

One approach would be to eliminate the corporate income tax, the employee-part payroll tax, or ultimately both. Both are regressive, anti-growth, and anti-small business. Replace them with a pollution tax, such as a per-ton tax on carbon or equivalent. Taxing pollution drives innovation and grows technology and manufacturing. It also puts more money in consumer's pockets, and gives them a choice: spend it on energy consumption, or on innovation.

Then, to assure that the benefits are global, use border adjustments to cut taxes more. Apply the same price on pollution to imported goods—including oil imports—so the price on domestic pollution does not inadvertently subsidize China, Venezuela, or Iran. *Use 100 percent of the proceeds to cut other taxes.*

Progressives tend to oppose reducing the corporate income tax, believing that taxing corporations is a good thing. They sometimes overlook the fact that large corporations often avoid the tax through permissible accounting practices, such as by shifting operations and profits outside the U.S. As a result, the corporate tax isn't paid by the companies progressives believe should be paying it. It most severely impacts small businesses and entrepreneurs, who have no easy way to escape the levy.

Better for small business, jobs, and the environment would be to eliminate the corporate tax, to drive manufacturing back to the U.S., where labor standards are strong, and liberate people to start businesses without facing a severe tax penalty.

Of course, politicians could still raise taxes, if they have the political courage to vote accordingly. But the political odds would finally be stacked against that. Today, taxes rise automatically. Inflation and prosperity combine to push people into higher and higher tax brackets, increasing government's share of total income. If we tax pollution instead of prosperity, this "automatic" process would begin to reverse. Politicians would be required to vote on any tax increases, again and again—and would incur the political risk of doing so. Voters would increasingly appreciate the benefits of taxing pollution instead of prosperity.

Taxing pollution would also enable the country to shift from highly polluting fuels, such as coal, to low-carbon, low sulfur oxide and low nitrogen oxide fuels, including the nation's newly abundant stores of natural gas. Regulating oil and gas production to meet environmental standards—or perhaps better, charging for every unit of pollution—can provide abundant energy to people and enterprises, and systematically draw more value from less fuel.

5

WIND DOWN SUBSIDIES

Stop subsidizing the past—wean us off
unnecessary spending.

In the postwar period, government established a complex web
of subsidies designed to rapidly increase production of food,
energy, water, and other commodities. These subsidies now cost
taxpayers as much as a trillion dollars a year, based on McKinsey
estimates. In a dynamic world, most of these subsidies do not
protect the health of the sectors they were originally intended to
support—instead, they shield them from change, and slow the
process of innovation. Gradually reducing these subsidies will
enable these sectors to grow more innovative and diversified.
They will replace the illusion of low prices—paid for with higher
taxes and deficits—with genuinely lower costs as innovators
find ways to create and add value.

For example, to meet rising population and income levels,
America and the world need to increase global food production
by 60 percent by 2050, and nearly all of that new total will need
to be regenerative—restoring our soils and cleaning our
waterways in the process. For the American farmer, the increase
in demand is already translating to record prices, but the
heartland is held back from capturing the additional gain from
regenerative methods—up to three times the profits per acre
and 30 percent higher yields during drought—because of federal
policy set in 1972 that favors a few standardized crops grown in
massive quantity.

Politics as usual would generally seek to meet this 60 percent increase in production by increasing subsidies for the biggest crops we already grow. But the costs of these subsidies is already too high. A new approach is needed, one that will help the agricultural sector diversify naturally, creating more value across a wider range of products and services, creating opportunities for large and small operators alike.

It is time to restore America's heartland. Instead of depleting soils and polluting rivers, the country can reduce tax and regulatory barriers to modern methods that will bring more land into cultivation, keep families on the land, and build regional food systems that keep more money circulating in local economies.

6

INCREASE RESEARCH

Fund basic and applied research, to drive innovation and productivity breakthroughs.

Government has a decided advantage over the private sector in at least one major area: research. According to David B. Audretsch, an economist at Indiana University, "Research and development (by government) unequivocally pays off economically."[28]

Government R&D plays a vital role in developing knowledge that can be applied later by individuals and companies, to create value across multiple sectors, sometimes quickly but often years later. A report by the National Research Council calculated that government R&D in eight computing technologies generated nearly $500 billion in revenue for 30 well-known corporations.

If that is the case, shouldn't those 30 companies pay for the research? Perhaps. But there are many systemic reasons that, when it comes to basic and applied research, government may be far more capable than the private sector of making sensible long-term investments with broad positive returns to society as a whole.

Research, especially basic research, generally produces large external effects, spillovers and "positive externalities" that can

---

28   http://www.nytimes.com/2012/10/07/technology/making-the-case-for-a-government-hand-in-research.html?_r=0

lead to benefits and applications for a wide array of individuals, firms, and communities.

But private firms seldom make investments in basic research, because they cannot "own" and accrue a large enough share of the dispersed benefits to justify their investments. Instead, they focus on applying the results of basic and applied research, to develop products and services with clearer and more predictable commercial applications.

From a societal perspective, private firms may underinvest in basic and applied research for several reasons.

First, results of basic research are uncertain.

Second, the time horizon for generating benefits is often long.

Third, the sectors benefited are usually not known in advance, and thus may benefit without paying the associated costs. Fourth, the benefits are often so dispersed, and the effects so intermixed with other causative factors, that the beneficiaries are hard to identify.

The purpose of *basic research* in physics, for example, is to make discoveries about the qualities of elementary particles and their combinations, even when commercial applications may be impossible to predict in advance. Private companies or even consortia rarely make these kinds of research investments, preferring those with a clear path of development that leads to applications for the funders.

The purpose of *applied research* in, for example, delivery vehicles for new pharmaceuticals is a step closer to commercialization because it seeks to develop scientific knowledge for a specific sectoral application.

But the benefits of a particular innovation are difficult to predict, and likely to accrue to a host of other sectors that do not contribute to the research. Private firms and consortia may support this research if they pay off to their sector is sufficient, but they will underinvest overall, because the returns for private firms do not encompass the social and economic benefits that research might bring to others.

Development applies scientific knowledge to create specific products and services for the marketplace. The private sector has more of an incentive to invest in development activities than in basic or applied research, primarily because a significant share of the benefits of the development accrue to the funder, through returns from users in the marketplace.

Since 1953, federal spending for R&D has grown, on average, about as fast as the overall economy, peaking at 2 percent of GDP in 1964, and declining in most years thereafter.

About half of this total has been for defense R&D, and half for a wide range of non-defense purposes. The defense portion is an example of "mission-based" R&D, because it focuses on developing specific products for which the U.S. government is the principle buyer.

The federal government funds about half of all research in the United States but only 17 percent of development.

Roughly 85-90 percent of federal non-defense R&D is for basic or applied research; under 15 percent is for development.

Private sector R&D is at least 80 percent dedicated to development. By contrast, federal defense spending is about 80 percent for development.

The best returns on government R&D investments tend to come from basic and applied research conducted at academic institutions. Studies show that average returns from that spending exceed the returns likely had the funds been put to other uses. The returns are also higher on research that reaches across disciplines for new ideas and tools, which would suggest that supporting research over a wide range of scientific fields is an important element in generating an economic return from federal research funding.[29]

In addition, some scholars argue that social returns are also high for federal development spending with wide applications across multiple sectors. The idea is not for government to "pick winners," but to target broader sectors for productivity improvements. Robert D. Adkison, coauthor with Stephen J. Ezell of "Innovation Economics: The Race for Global Advantage" (Yale University Press), proposes that the U.S. emulate Germany's network of 60 Fraunhofer Institutes, financed 70 percent by business and 30 percent by government. The institutes, he says, help bring new technologies to market, and are part of the reason Germany has a strong manufacturing sector even though its factory workers are paid 40 percent higher than those in the U.S.

---

29 http://www.cbo.gov/sites/default/files/cbofiles/ftpdocs/82xx/doc8221/06-18-research.pdf

7

PROTECT AIR, WATER, AND LAND

Reduce environmental and climate risks, and use the market to foster conservation and stewardship.

Don't socialize the costs of pollution. Foster conservation and stewardship, through laws and regulations that assure that people and companies "own" their positive and negative environmental impacts. If every unit of pollution imposes a cost, and every reduction delivers a benefit, the costs will be systematically reduced.

The six principles discussed so far have illustrated a number of market-based approaches that foster both prosperity and sustainability.

"The nation behaves well if it treats the Natural Resources as assets, which it must turn over to the next generation increased."

- Theodore Roosevelt

8

RENEW BIG CITIES, SMALL TOWNS, AND COMMUNITIES

Reform outdated codes and remove barriers to micro-entrepreneurship and the sharing economy to revitalize big cities, small towns, and local communities.

The post-World War II economy favored industrial mass production in centralized factories set far away from homes. People were drawn away from big cities and small towns, into fast-growing suburbs where factory and office workers lived. The results were largely positive—productivity drove prosperity, a major benefit that required acceptance of big institutions, standardized social roles, segregated work and home lives, and a declining sense of connection and community.

Today, we have the opportunity to reintegrate the siloed lifestyles of recent generations, to bring together the worlds of home and work, production and consumption, masculine and feminine, secular and sacred that were separated in the last economy. The economy has moved beyond this suburban-focused standardization. People have new opportunities to contribute in much more diverse ways. They no longer need to fit in rigid mass manufacturing models. They do not all need to live in suburbs where homes and lives tend toward the identical.

It is time to draw people back into small towns and big cities, bring diversity and a sense of community and place to the suburbs, and integrate lives in ways that not only stretch resources further, but bring people closer. To do so, it is now prudent to ease away from the rigid 1950's era codes and zoning laws that compelled home builders and buyers to inhabit centralized standardized suburbs in which diversity and walkability is sacrificed in favor of dependence on automobiles, strip malls, and standardized ethnic, racial, and gender roles.

At the local and state level, eliminate the rigid codes and zoning laws that were designed for generic automobile-dependent suburban growth in the 1950s and 1960s. Replace them with updated, adaptive, resilient approaches that foster a diverse array of small towns, healthy neighborhoods, and big cities, where people are able to find their place and contribute their best.

Remove the barriers to small scale capitalism, micro-entrepreneurship, and the sharing economy that is one of the richest sources of entrepreneurship, offering opportunities for busy parents whose lives don't accommodate the rigid old 8-5 commuter lifestyle. Change the burdensome licensing, zoning, hotel, and commercial mandates that prevent homesharing, carsharing, child care, office hubs, and myriad other opportunities for people to build community and trade energy. People don't need to be forced to use intermediaries to meet their basic needs. When 90 percent of cars have empty seats, when half of homes have extra rooms, when office equipment that could serve 100 serves only one, we waste money and miss opportunities to connect.

Establish safe harbor laws that protect small microenterprises from local, state, and federal mandates meant for large enterprises, so that creative people are free to harness their own capital—their knowledge and possessions—to serve needs and pay bills. Community-grown enterprises plant seeds of innovation that grow value for all.

It is time once again to foster community and share resources, and one necessary step is to sunset the outdated codes and zoning and licensing laws that artificially subsidize and support it. American tastes have changed from the splendid isolation of the suburbs to what advocates are calling the "five-minute lifestyle"—work, school, transit, doctors, dining, playgrounds, entertainment all within a five-minute walk of the front door. From 2014 to 2029, baby boomers and their children, the millennial generation, will converge in the housing marketplace—seeking smaller homes in walkable, service-rich, transit-oriented communities. Already, 56 percent of Americans seek this lifestyle in their next housing purchase. That's roughly three times the demand for such housing after World War II.

The motivations are common across the country. Boomers are downsizing and working longer, and they fear losing their keys in the car-dependent suburbs. Millennials were raised in the isolated suburbs of the 1980s and 1990s, and 77 percent never want to go back. Prices have already flipped, with exurban property values dropping while those in walkable neighborhoods are spiking. Yet legacy federal policies—from transportation funding to housing subsidies—remain geared toward the Cold War imperative of population dispersion and exploitation of the housing shortage, and they are stifling that demand.

It is not only the United States that needs to get its house in order. Within all regional-scale economic areas, the country will work with the global partnership to promote a mode of development that results in prosperity, security, and sustainability for their citizens.

Export-led growth and resource-extraction strategies will no longer suffice. Housing, agriculture, and resource productivity will be the drivers of sustainable economic development, producing jobs, investment, and government revenue. While each region will have a unique starting point, global income convergence will unleash substantial trade opportunities as each region develops robust internal markets. Solutions pioneered in one region will find markets in others. As multiple regions create advanced manufacturing capability, global supply chains will become more dynamic and resilient.

9

REFORM GOVERNANCE

Move beyond gridlock, toward government that
is democratic, functional, and free.

Too often, the governing institutions that assure representative
democracy have been shaped and constrained to support a
variety of uncoordinated status-quo interests, from incumbent
legislators to industrial and labor interests, to protect their
power and immunize the system against change.

When lawmakers, often from a single party, are able to
gerrymander districts to protect incumbents and establish long-
term control by a single party; when rules for political
contributions are parsed in ways intended to enhance or reduce
the influence of particular constituencies and institutions; when
small individual contributions are buried beneath an avalanche
of unlimited quasi-independent contributions; when
corporations and unions are compelled to spend ever-more on
campaign contributions simply to ensure access to lawmakers;
when the judicial system is partisanized and politicized to
support popular prejudices over constitutional principles; when
lawmakers find they have less independent power than lobbyists
and legislative staff who face no term limits; then the principles
of democracy gradually erode into the reality of a system biased
in favor of the past and against future.

Just as America would never fight a 21st-century war with
rusted weapons from the Korean War-era, it should not govern
today with institutions devised for a bygone era and often

burdened by dependencies that prevent them from adapting to new realities. The Founding Fathers established a constitution that allows for the adaptation of the institutions of government to the knowledge, threats, and opportunities confronting each generation. Americans should make use of that foresight.

At the state level, democracy is partly a fiction when lawmakers from either party map legislative districts to protect incumbents and create single-party districts. The process makes voting only half-functional, and favors extreme and divisive candidates over those that can unite their constituents behind them. New redistricting rules need to be advanced under which citizen or judicial commissions design districts to be genuinely representative and competitive. Open primary systems can give voters greater choice and influence on the outcome of elections.

At the federal level, today's executive branch was largely designed to support the country through the Cold War, and it is misaligned to the requirements of the 21st century. The U.S. national security establishment can barely see the challenges of today, let alone predict the crises of tomorrow. America's domestic departments are designed to support an economic strategy that is now weakening the country. Congress is supposed to oversee this system, but it too cannot rise above the noise. The White House, meanwhile, has not maintained a robust strategic capacity since 1961.

Just as the 1947 National Security Act adapted the U.S. national security establishment to take on the Cold War, the country will adapt again to implement and manage this strategy. It will reorganize agencies and departments to execute the elements of this strategy. Congress will be encouraged to align its oversight committees to the new federal departments.

In peacetime, U.S. foreign-policy agencies—providing defense, diplomacy, development, and intelligence—will align around one map and fall under integrated civilian control at the global, regional, and country levels. Domestically, the United States will clear out the economic policies of the past and ensure that housing, agriculture, and resource productivity are incentivized and regulated to ensure fair, robust, and open markets with strong consumer protections.

10

INCLUDE EVERYONE

Broadly disseminate both freedom and responsibility. Celebrate the capacities of all people in all their diversity, respecting and welcoming women and men, gay and straight, immigrants new and old, minorities and majorities to contribute fully, without prejudice.

The mid-20th century economy favored institutions and jobs in which people were siloed in narrow categories where their generic group traits could be harnessed. Instead of being able to express themselves as individuals, people were stereotyped based on generic models of how their groups should behave—whether or not they fit the norms. Men were seen to be physically stronger and more oriented to top-down management controls, so they were assigned roles in which those qualities were emphasized, and others discouraged. Women were seen to be more emotionally nurturing and oriented to collaborative problem-solving, so women were limited to roles in the home and community, caring for children and fostering connection. Certain racial and ethnic groups were assigned to traditional roles, prevented sometimes by law or cultural norms and prejudices from pursuing positions deemed to be for a different group.

Conformity was function from the perspective of industrial production. People could fill generic roles in factories, offices, farms, and the service sector, enabling efficient rote productivity. The tradeoff may have been worthwhile, since the productive gains enabled higher pay and better working conditions on average. But today, that tradeoff is no longer necessary. In a digital economy, people prosper not so much by fitting into a social stereotype, but by being themselves, and offering their distinctive natures and capacities.

Instead of stereotypes that lock us into pre-assigned roles, we become distinctive individuals, within distinctive groups. Our differences become not handicaps to be hidden or denied, but strengths that we add to enrich our communities. Women and men, gay and straight, minority and majority, left and right exist not as separate siloes to be kept apart, but rich, internally diversified, overlapping sets of qualities that foster innovation and growth, at the individual and community level.

Cultural and legal norms need to evolve to support a diverse yet cohesive and inclusive society, an all-in culture where competition and cooperation coexist; where by being themselves, people find the roles that they fill distinctively; where diversity fosters unity as people bring together their individual strengths to form functional wholes; where people of specific ethnic, gender, national, and sexual orientations face no institutional barriers to full and equal participation in American life.

These ten innovation principles will create wealth and jobs, drive technological innovation, renew small towns and big cities, reduce pollution, help wean the world off coal, oil and other carbon-based fuels, and create the value we need to pay off our debts and grow genuinely prosperous. It requires zero net tax increases.

An Innovation Nation will also help move us beyond the need for rigid command-and-control regulations to crudely internalize the negative externalities of economic activity. By pricing pollution and waste, we reduce externalities automatically, more closely aligning private profit with public good.

An Innovation Nation will reduce depletion of strategic and nonrenewable resources, without requiring that we sacrifice physical comfort or the pursuit of happiness. It will drive technology change. It will help rebuild and transform our manufacturing sector by improving efficiency and productivity, adding tremendous value through the design and information content of manufactured products. It will harness what America does best—innovation—and help strengthen our economy for our coming race with China.

An Innovation Nation will also cut the flow of dollars to Middle East and Latin American dictators. This will reduce the chances of conflict and the risk that our sons and daughters will have to experience the perils of war.

An Innovation Nation would also pursue other opportunities where the Left and Right to join forces. These opportunities might include health care *systems* that empower, enable, and reward people to stay healthy, and channel part of the gain from that to assist those who face potentially catastrophic health challenges. Systems that outperform standardization and consolidation, by encouraging specialization and integration, with smaller practices that continuously improve and master their specialties, so they can deliver the best results at the lowest cost.

These opportunities might also include education *systems* with robust, adaptive schools available to all, that foster knowledge and learning through small schools focused on developing their specialties, within a robust integrated market, so parents and students have access to different curricula to match different aptitudes and interests. Systems that can outperform big, consolidated programs and provide the impetus for continuous improvement that can deliver the best results at the lowest cost and make American schools the best in the world.

It is time for politics to catch up with change. The economy of the last century was dominated by large relatively generic industrial interests, like General Motors, Standard Brands, General Electric, and Standard Oil. They helped unleash the prosperity that has led to a new generation of companies founded more on information and telecommunications technology. These in turn have helped empower individuals to liberate themselves from top-down institutions, and create value that reflects their unique capacities.

Innovation is Transpartisan:

A Right-to-Left Alliance for the 21st Century

"Why do the politicians and the media figures want us to hate each other? It's pervasive on both sides of the aisle. There's something going on. I argue that it's the politics of hate. It's very profitable for them to have us hate one another. When I go to Washington D.C., the vast majority of staff and electeds I meet with – they want me to hate the other side. But I just don't come from that place. I think when we come from a place where we empathize and care for the other side, we're more likely to find that common ground."

- Tea Party Patriots co-founder Mark Meckler,
in conversation with
Move-On co-founder Joan Blades[30]

The Republican and Democratic Parties symbolically represent the two idealized roles of American parents. The Republicans are the nation's father figure. The Democrats are the nation's mother figure.

In a healthy union, these two work together to provide what the family needs. The feminine represents purpose—the "why"—while the masculine represents power—the "how." In

---

30   http://www.upworthy.com/a-former-tea-party-patriot-gives-a-speech-that-will-make-progressives-stand-up-a

the real world, mothers and fathers each apply both masculine and feminine qualities. But the mother tends to be the connective force, representing the higher purpose of the family, as a single unit that shares love and support for one another. The father, on the other hand, represents the power that is exerted to advance that purpose. The masculine serves the feminine; power serves purpose.

Of course, neither party genuinely advances its role. Each has been co-opted by the realities of day-to-day politics. Each gives rhetorical voice to its respective parental role. But each adopts positions that reflect politically powerful interests—often, the very same interests. Then, each explains its positions using the terms that appeal to its base.

For example, both major parties favor an increase in government size, power, and spending. They each advance tax loopholes and subsidies for favored industries, associations, unions, and interest groups. Democrats may rhetorically seek to pay for them with higher direct taxes; Republicans may rhetorically oppose new overt taxes but favor higher back-door taxes—deficit spending. Since it is easier to spend money than collect it, debt explodes.

The result is an economy that has become dangerously dependent on government stimulus, as its primary means to drive growth. Rather than creating value, through innovation and entrepreneurship, we drive consumption, by increasing the flow of dollars through the economy. This extends Keynesianism a bridge too far: Keynes never intended his general theory to be sole driver of long-term prosperity.

Groups ranging from the Tea Party on the right to Move-On on the left are beginning to see through the charade, however, and to demand that each party adhere more honestly to its principles. This frustrates the official major party leaders, who insist that their party is making pragmatic choices, within a tough political environment, and doing its best to advance its underlying principles.

Unfortunately for the nation, this leaves us paralyzed, and places our prosperity and democracy at risk.

The Republican and Democratic parties and some of their ideological groups represent the two halves of the larger system America needs in order to create new value.

Unfortunately, those who want to weave these two halves together are facing a very high barrier. Each of our major parties is now dominated by vested interests who gain from gridlock and are threatened by change. They know how to craft their political arguments to win the support of ideologues, and convince them that the other party is intrinsically evil and must be vanquished. These true believers can impose the political equivalent of capital punishment on politicians who seek to collaborate with the evil enemy. This is an effective strategy, since an ambitious public official usually sees the loss of an election as a fate worse than death.

As a consequence, we have alternated between the policies of an interest group dependent Right and Left for two generations. This has finally left us paralyzed, frozen in place, even in the face of potentially disastrous economic and ecological consequences. The only beneficiaries are vested interests—in other words, the old institutions that used to represent all of us, and still often do, but in narrow and non-sustainable ways. Before we can move forward, we must look at ourselves, to see how our interests have changed. Then we must look to the Left and to the Right, and see how their core principles can new serve us in new ways.

"After all," as transpartisan writer Charles Wheelan says, "there is a lot to like about the Republicans: a belief in personal responsibility, a respect for markets and the forces of wealth creation, an understanding of the economic costs of taxation and regulation, and a healthy skepticism of what government can and cannot accomplish. And there is a lot to like about the Democrats: a concern for working people, a commitment to a strong social safety net, an impressive record of social tolerance, a long-standing concern for the environment, and a recognition that government can play a crucial role in protecting us from the most egregious abuses of capitalism. But neither party is putting its best foot forward right now."[31]

That is putting it mildly. The country cannot delay. For a few short years, we have a window in which we can choose a highly prosperous 21st century, but that window will close. It is time once more to lead the world through difficult change.

The United States must first get its own house in order. We will renew our industrial base and manufacturing sector, cultivate new paths to a new American Dream, and lead the world by example while defining the future and inspiring greatness. And we will do all this while emerging from an economic depression that is wasting our most precious resource—the creativity and enterprise of our people.

It is, as the great strategist George Kennan understood, the truest test of America's worth as a nation. And while some might say U.S. politics are not up to the task, the great purposes for which America's founders brought forward the United States endure: liberty, justice, the common defense, and the general welfare—not only for ourselves, but also for future generations. These are the sacred goals of the United States, and they are calling a new generation to author a bold and

---

31 http://www.centristproject.org/the_big_idea; and Charles Wheelan, The Centrist Manifesto, W. W. Norton, 2013. ISBN 0-393-34687-0

uncompromising future that remains prosperous, secure, and resilient.

Stepping only to the right, or only to the left, we walk in circles. But stepping right, then left, then right and left again, we move ahead. In an Innovation Nation, the Right and Left can walk together, each contributing core principles that together bring genuine long-term prosperity.

> *"No one in America is born a Democrat or a Republican. We are born Americans. No one comes to this country to become a Democrat or a Republican. We come here to be Americans. Our common purpose is to fully unleash the potential of every individual. The United States is in the full potential business. It is time to get to work, and advance our potential."*
>
> - Roy Spence, co-founder, GSDM, and a "Clinton Democrat"

ABOUT THE AUTHOR

Author Bill Shireman is a lifelong Republican, serial entrepreneur, and well-known environmental advocate. As a founding director of the Republican Leadership Network, he seeks to advance systemic market-based alternatives to centralized command-and-control mandates often initially preferred by big government, big business, and big social and environmental advocacy organizations. As President and CEO of Future 500, he places himself between groups that love to hate and demonize each other: the right and left, Rush Limbaugh conservatives and Michael Moore progressives, and above all, the world's best-known companies and most impassioned activist groups. With his dedicated colleagues, Shireman has successfully united business and civic leaders behind systems-based solutions that actually work, to clean up the environment, recycle resources, promote human rights, and help solve some of the world's most challenging problems. He believes those solutions can be found in the principles that underlie the two most innovative systems on the planet: the rainforest and the economy – free-flowing markets and free-flowing ecosystems.

* * *

affinitypressbooks.com

Made in the USA
San Bernardino, CA
28 October 2014